D0988455

# THE
# TENANT'S
# SURVIVAL
# GUIDE

NEWHAM LIBRARIES

01817420

*If you want to know how. . .*

**The Landlord's Survival Guide**
*The truly practical insider handbook for all private landlords*

**The Beginner's Guide to Property investment**
*The ultimate handbook for first-time buyers
and would-be property investors*

**How Safe is Your Home?**
*Expert advice that will reduce
the risk of you being burgled*

**Planning and Creating Your First Garden**
*A step-by-step guide to designing your garden –
whatever your experience and knowledge*

**howto**books

Send for a free copy of the latest catalogue to:

How To Books
Spring Hill House, Spring Hill Road,
Begbroke, Oxford OX5 1RX. United Kingdom.
info@howtobooks.co.uk
www.howtobooks.co.uk

# THE
# TENANT'S
# SURVIVAL
# GUIDE

### ESSENTIAL READING FOR PROSPECTIVE TENANTS
### AND THOSE ALREADY IN RENTED ACCOMMODATION

# LESLEY HENDERSON

**howto**books

| NEWHAM LIBRARY LEISURE SERVICE | |
|---|---|
| 01817420 | |
| HJ | 10/12/2007 |
| 346.420434 | |
| NHBG | |

Published by How To Books Ltd
Spring Hill House, Spring Hill Road
Begbroke, Oxford OX5 1RX. United Kingdom
Tel: (01865) 375794. Fax: (01865) 379162
info@howtobooks.co.uk
www.howtobooks.co.uk

*The Tenant's Survival Guide* is designed to assist private tenants in England and Wales. However, it cannot be construed and is not purported to be in any instance a substitute for legal advice. In situations concerning legal uncertainties in relation to personal tenant and landlord liabilities, past, present and future, a solicitor must be consulted. While every effort has been made to ensure that the information contained herein is accurate, neither the publisher nor the author can accept liability for any errors, nor any consequences legal or otherwise taken as a result of reading or the practical adherence to the proposals contained within this book.

The right of Lesley Henderson to be identified as author of this work has been asserted by her in accordance with the Copyright, Designs and Patents Act 1988.

© **2007 Lesley Henderson**

British Library Cataloguing in Publication Data
A catalogue record for this book is available from the British Library

ISBN 978 1 84528 231 8

Cover illustration by David Mostyn
Cover design by Baseline Arts, Oxford
Produced for How To Books by Deer Park Productions, Tavistock, Devon
Typeset by PDQ Typesetting, Newcastle-under-Lyme, Staffs.
Printed and bound by Bell & Bain Ltd, Glasgow

NOTE: The material contained in this book is set out in good faith for general guidance and no liability can be accepted for loss or expense incurred as a result of relying in particular circumstances on statements made in the book. The laws and regulations are complex and liable to change, and readers should check the current position with the relevant authorities before making personal arrangements.

# Contents

# Preface

Having worked in the lettings industry for most of my adult life, I have become keenly aware that practical information for tenants is not circulating well. And that's putting it mildly!

I can't think of another single industry or service that comes close to the rental sector for disputes or misunderstandings, despite its importance let alone its economic clout. The cost of an *average* rental in South East England will cost tenants as much as a pretty decent car *every single year*. Even further afield, most tenants are still paying between a third and a half of everything they earn to keep a rented roof over their heads. However... what all tenants need to understand from the beginning is that they are often *not* even the customers in transactions that involve agencies.

What do I mean? Well, let's buy a chocolate bar in, say, Woolworths. Pay 40 pence and you become the customer. Along with all the consumer protections that come with *being* a customer. Let's take another example and buy that car from a reputable dealership. Clearly, again, you hand over the cash and thus become the customer. Simple.

Not so for the huge number of tenants who rent property via agencies. In the overwhelming majority of instances, the letting agent's customer is *the landlord* − *not* the tenant. And, like any other business, agencies respond to the needs of their customers − who unfortunately in this case are not the ones handing over all that money each month. Far too often the tenants' needs get completely lost in this type of arrangement.

It's an interesting anomaly that the most expensive purchase of a tenant's year is often the very one over which they'll have little or no control.

> It's a harsh lesson that tenants need to get to grips with. It's one that should inform how *every* tenant decides to spend all that hard earned cash each month.

The relationship between a tenant and a landlord direct *can* – in many instances – be easier to manage. You are, much more effectively, the customer here and, as a majority of landlords still don't use agencies for all sorts of reasons, this means that a huge number of tenants and landlords do business without the expense of middlemen. However, such direct relationships can sometimes lead to another, quite different set of problems for tenants to deal with.

In fact, the *real* double blind in letting/rentals is that tenants are always the ones left struggling to know where they stand, while also being the ones who pay handsomely for the privilege.

Just one more thing. Tenants in England and Wales (with some rare exceptions explained later) have precious few meaningful rights once something called The Fixed Term comes to an end. (Read Lesson on leases. You'll already know this better as the original length of the agreement.) Once that extremely limited period of legal protection ends, it's no exaggeration to say that a tenant's rights could be balanced on the proverbial pinhead.

## Welcome to the world of the modern tenant

No guide can change Housing Legislation that governs how you rent, from whom, for how long, let alone how much it all costs. What it *can* do is help you to negotiate your way through some very expensive and quite complex contracts. It can help you to understand them and their hidden consequences. It will teach you how they operate and what to watch for in the small print, and show you where your protections do exist – and where they don't. It can point out pitfalls and help you find your way around some of them.

Plus, it explains what a reasonable landlord *can and will insist on* to protect their own, very considerable interests.

I've illuminated a few tricks of the trade so you don't get stung too often. I've also included details on some new and very interesting legislation covering **rental deposits** that since April 2007 affect almost all landlords/agents and tenants too. I've also given you a flavour of other new laws that should soon, with luck, help in reducing dangerous housing conditions that can so often affect sharers on tight budgets. In short, spending a bit of time reading here should make a real difference to your everyday life as a tenant.

Now for the reality check. If *I* were going to hand over to a virtual stranger the kind of money that it takes to set up an average tenancy (and *never* forget that you only met this landlord/agent yesterday) then I'd want some realistic advice on what to expect.

Good and bad practice is widespread. Tenants with little experience can't possibly just guess and get it right. So try reading the whole of this guide. It shouldn't take long and its style is lighthearted and conversational. I've even thrown in a few true stories to make you laugh (or cry).

Although it's often claimed that tenants have 'rights' under a variety of Housing Acts, Common Law, and Consumer Protection Acts, in reality this protection is about as much use as a chocolate teapot for anyone with six months' security of tenure under an Assured Shorthold lease, which is what you'll be getting as a modern tenant. By the time any action can be taken to enforce safety or contract, landlords or agents may have decided to *quite legally* remove what they consider to be 'troublesome tenants'. It's a right that they do have in law and bad landlords/agents use it all too often to 'control' very legitimate tenant concerns.

However, do remember that, out there in this *huge* marketplace are thousands of hard working, fair minded landlords who treat their tenants in just the way that any other customer would expect. It's your job as a tenant to learn how to find yourself one of the majority and, frankly, how to steer clear of the rest.

By providing clear information, what you read here should help you to learn what to look for, what to try avoiding, how to conduct your tenancy, and with luck, leave with your deposit intact. I also provide access points to other useful and reliable sources of information to help build on what I've incorporated here. It should also explain why rushing to sign a contract that you don't understand (or even bother to read!) can often be a grave a mistake.

This guide is not intended to be a legal manual, but a practical one – for when the law is as ineffective as it is for the vast majority of tenants, practicality rather than theory is what will help you most.

# Introduction

Over the past several years there has been an unprecedented range of changes to Housing Law, which massively affects how tenancies operate in England and Wales (with more important changes still coming courtesy of the new 2004 legislation – this time you'll be relieved to read, designed mainly to protect *tenants* rather than investors).

The most significant of these first changes was undoubtedly the introduction in 1988 of **assured shorthold** leases. These leases mean exactly what they suggest. Shorthold says it all. These tenancies are *not* permanent. They *can* become longer term, but only if the landlord is happy with the way that a tenancy is running. Once your initial protections run out, everything depends on the way you behave as a tenant.

Until the introduction of assured shortholds, almost all tenancies required a landlord to prove (to a court) that s/he had good enough legal reasons for requiring the tenancy to be terminated: reasons like damage, antisocial conduct or unpaid rent. The introduction of **assured shorthold tenancies** means that any landlord who decides to terminate a tenancy after a short period may do so for no legal reason whatever. Landlords (or their agents) *don't need* any particular reason to ask for their property back once the first 'fixed term' has expired. Of course, that doesn't mean they can simply change the locks – both sides have processes to go through to end tenancies – but in effect landlords have the key to the car, their foot on the throttle and full control of the brakes. Modern tenants remain fare paying passengers *at all times*.

## The 'fixed term'

Almost, but not quite all, modern leases begin with a **fixed term**. This is the original length of time agreed to offer a lease for and it will normally be six months.

Now, this original fixed term *matters*. Beyond that, tenants have no control over the length of time for which they will be able to continue their contract. Together with other far-reaching changes, this legislation has utterly transformed the lettings industry. (Fixed Terms are explained in much more detail in Lesson 1.)

These legal transformations have both positive and negative effects for tenants. There has been a genuine upturn in the supply of rented housing, and we can forget about past shortages. Nowadays, when higher education and shorter-term employment contracts mean we all have to move around much more than we ever did before, this increased supply is absolutely vital.

However, while everyone welcomes the increased supply and choice, gone also are the days when tenancies lasted for as long as the tenant wanted, so long as the contract terms were not breached. The whole way in which we occupy rented property has changed beyond all recognition. And that has proved to be a very mixed blessing for tenants.

'Market rents' have replaced 'fair rents', which at least offered some control on costs. Tight contracts, in which every detail of tenant conduct is clearly laid out, are now commonplace. Agencies have been rapidly established to service this growing sector and their sole reason for existence is to make profits at every stage of the rental process. Being a tenant is now vastly more costly and infinitely less secure than it has been for decades (and indeed *still is* in many parts of the world where rentals are permanent lifestyles).

These changes affect every single aspect of being a tenant in England and Wales.

## What difference does this make to me?

The first difference this has made is that if you do want to be a tenant, you will have no difficulty in finding something to rent. You may even be lucky enough to find a local glut in your price range. However, the climate in which you rent has been utterly transformed. The introduction of assured shorthold leases has removed any security of tenure beyond that first 'fixed term'. The landlord's guaranteed 'no fault' right to repossession has restricted tenants enormously. Every player – landlords, agents and tenants – now knows that if tenants complain their lease need not last beyond the legal minimum, and this is usually only six short months.

The difference that this has made is absolutely critical. Tenants now enter a highly commercialised, expensive market, in the certain knowledge that if they have even the most reasonable cause for complaint, they may, for no other reason than raising a problem, be asked to leave their home. We have entered uncharted waters where tenants – even those with very *genuine* problems with their accommodation – don't feel confident enough to complain about a thing.

It is very easy for people (invariably home owners) to shrug their shoulders, and wonder why you should mind moving on if you're not happy? However, moving is expensive, and unsettling, whether you're a tenant or an owner-occupier. Being told to leave a property that you have dutifully paid rent on and cared for because you complained about something reasonable is a bitter pill to swallow for most tenants.

The double irony remains that your single largest expense, i.e. your home, should be the one thing that you are unable to raise any legitimate concerns about.

### WARNING ANECDOTE

I know of one young couple with a baby who lived for four months with no cooker because their agent made it clear that the landlord would not renew their lease if any repair accounts were submitted, 'on principle'!

Another whose bathroom ceiling collapsed, leaving tenants upstairs and downstairs staring at one another's personal habits through the floorboards. And still the landlord wouldn't pay for a repair!

Why? Because they could. Because tenants' security is tenuous and tenants who complain are often simply asked to leave 'on principle'.

The Housing Acts 1988 may have solved the problems of under-supply, but they have, in reality, created another, quite different set of problems that place far too much control over lifestyles in the hands of virtual strangers, yet offer absolutely no quality control or meaningful safeguards to tenants who have genuine problems. This is unlikely to change. That is why tenants need to know what to look for, because well cared for units simply cause less areas of friction.

Interestingly, problems in the seventies and eighties were genuinely experienced by landlords, who – even when they had the most appalling problems with their tenants – found it almost impossible to regain possession of their property. A completely different type of problem now exists, this time for tenants who, despite paying high rents, and signing very stringent contracts, find it is their turn to be virtually powerless.

## What should I do to protect my interests?

In this highly commercial market, where rights are limited, tenants need to know what to look for, not only in the property itself, but also in its management (agent or landlord). Ideally tenants need to be well informed *before they ever sign* a contract.

Inexperienced tenants (and they form the majority) need to learn how to assess and protect their own interests quickly and efficiently. Property is now very expensive to rent and good units often go very quickly in a market where they are still at a premium. Learning what to look for and why is now an essential part of being a tenant.

## How will *The Tenant's Survival Guide* help me?

The aim of the guide is primarily to show you how to establish a sensible framework within which both you and your landlord can operate in harmony. It sets out not only what you can expect from your landlord or agent, but also what they can reasonably expect from you. That will help you to recognise what should concern you, and show you some easy, practical ways to protect your own interests.

You may find some of the guide alarming, some of it amusing, but all of it will help you negotiate the realities of being a private tenant today. Throughout the guide you will find numerous anecdotes from landlords and tenants, which have been used to illustrate potential pitfalls. These will help you to learn from the past misfortunes of others (there's no substitute for experience, even if it's someone else's!). None of these is invented; as a service we generate enough horror stories to set anyone's teeth on edge without the help of fiction.

### *What is in this* Tenant's Survival Guide?

Most local authorities, Citizens' Advice Bureaux and tenancy advisory groups have already produced small, quite helpful pamphlets for tenants. They do however tend to concentrate on clear areas like major disrepair (the roof fell in), illegal eviction (suitcases in the front garden) and other forms of major harassment. Many also still include information on tenancies, which are no longer likely to be issued, as these booklets are intended to cover the whole spectrum of tenancy problems and there are still a surprising number of regulated tenants with old style contracts, still running out there in the marketplace.

*The Tenant's Survival Guide* is designed quite specifically to cover only Assured Shorthold Tenants, or those who have been offered 'licences to occupy'. It is able therefore to concentrate on the vast majority of modern tenants with little or no security of tenure and very few rights to enforce. Because, despite these being the overwhelming majority of tenancies, problem-solving advice for this huge and growing army of tenants is usually brief. It is often also accompanied by a warning that you have very little security – and you might not want to enforce what limited rights you do have because this could very well result in a legal request to vacate.

> Fewer rights mean that you need to know how to *avoid* problems because you will never be in a position to force anyone to rectify them.

It is much harder to advise people when they have very little legal redress. If you complain, or have a problem on an assured shorthold, and that lease is legitimately brought to an end, what has happened may be grossly unfair, but it is certainly not illegal!

Put simply, informed tenants will do well, and badly informed tenants will *struggle*. Believe me, landlords and agents have quickly learned how to manage under-informed tenants. The purpose of this guide is to give tenants access to a range of experience that agents and landlords already enjoy. Longer than a pamphlet (but shorter than *War and Peace*), this guide aims to help you both foresee and resolve the type of problems you are likely to be dealing with as a tenant with limited tenure. I've made it short, informative and practical. It is also a technical reference point, somewhere for you to look up specifics should a problem arise during your tenancy.

## Where else could I get advice?

I wish I could throw in a long list of resources here – but I can't. It has been remarkably difficult for tenants to actually get hold of useful advice about these types of tenancies. Advice on assured shortholds is limited; because your *rights* are limited. There's nothing else to say! These particular tenancies need a proactive, forewarned tenants. Tenants who know about their knock-on effects and have been advised about their consequences. Why? Because, as a tenant, you certainly can't exercise control over them.

The only other readily available source of information which tenants can access is legal advice. However, most of us (except in the most serious of instances) find this a very expensive option. Too often tenants realise that their position is insecure, and that their landlord is holding a considerable sum of *their* money (advance rent plus of course that deposit). For many, it is simply cheaper to cut their losses than to lose money fighting futile battles.

## Some final advice

Many private landlords provide high quality, safe and well-serviced properties. A minority are appalling, offering inadequate, overcrowded, and sometimes downright unsafe properties. And, of course, the overwhelming majority fall somewhere between the two.

Don't however forget that (even if it often doesn't feel that way), you are a *customer* of your landlord. It may well be your rent which will be paying the mortgage on a property. Your landlord may be acquiring a portfolio of properties, all funded by rental income. You may not have too many legal remedies available to you, but landlords and agencies cannot survive without tenants' revenue, because *you* fund our entire industry. The one thing that worries a modern landlord is an empty unit. This is the *only* card in your deck, so learn how to play it effectively. As always, a contract between two well informed parties based on mutual respect has a much greater chance of success than any other sort.

This guide should equip you well in your search for accommodation and help you resolve misunderstandings during tenancies without coming to blows. And always remember...

> Landlords and agents are well prepared – you need to ensure that they aren't the only parties who know what they are doing!

# Lesson 1

# Basic things to understand *before* you start renting

## How renting works

Tenants need some basic explanations about the contracts on offer and other associated but important issues. Most are touched on in Lesson 1 to get you started, then delved into more deeply in the relevant lessons. Just keep reading. This lesson will give you a pretty good idea of how renting/letting works long before you start signing contracts that you can't get out of.

For most tenants, their first step is to find out the going rate for properties that match their needs, in other words, how much what they want will actually cost them. Savvy tenants will check the papers, research online and visit agents to get a feel for how much money will be involved in what they're looking to rent. Landlords and agencies are, since the introduction of the Housing Acts 1988, allowed to effectively charge the local 'going rate' for all assured shorthold tenancies. There's therefore very little that most tenants can do to control costs but to shop carefully.

### Assured shorthold tenancies operate on 'market rents'

For more than a decade, control of rents has been a fairly hands off affair for officialdom. How much you're being asked to pay will usually be a combination of the local conditions, the state of the property and, of course, the price of local property versus how much you can afford to pay.

This is known as a 'market rent' (as opposed to the old strictly controlled 'fair rents' that − believe it or not − still apply to very old tenancies). Most of us should welcome this. 'Fair rents' contributed to the sharp decline in property to rent, whereas 'market rents' have encouraged a growth in supply, generating far more choice and availability. This is good news for tenants, but it has set costs spiralling.

### Rent assessment committees

There are still some very limited facilities, which tenants can use, but only in situations where they really believe that the rent they are being charged is basically outrageous – *way* beyond other similar units in their area. The Rent Assessment Committee (RAC) exists to exert some limited influence on totally excessive rent levels; but tenants should be very wary about making an application. Rent levels are often raised by this committee as well as reduced.

If you genuinely feel that the rent you are being charged is totally out of line with others in the same area, you can obtain details from your Citizens' Advice Bureau about where your local RAC is. Check thoroughly before you make an application. All RACs keep a public record of their decisions, which you can examine. If the difference is marginal they are unlikely to intervene, and you are likely to have irritated your landlord for no good reason. Don't expect a lease to run long with an agitated landlord.

Far better than taking on a property which you think is unreasonably priced, or worse still, one that you are going to have difficulty managing to pay for, is to look carefully at what is on offer in the area you need to live in, and rent something which you *can* afford.

## Understanding your 'fixed term'

I know it sounds like boring technical stuff, but every modern tenant needs to *really* understand the principal of fixed terms. This is the original duration of your lease written onto your assured shorthold lease. This fixed term is vitally important and is explained in more detail in Lesson 8.

> However, understand this right from the outset.
> Assured shorthold tenancies are, by their design, *temporary*.
> Tenants have *no* automatic *or* legal rights to stay beyond
> that original fixed term.

Of course, that doesn't mean that all tenancies end on the dot of their fixed term by any stretch. Many run on for years, with or without much alteration in terms. Nor does it mean that a landlord/agent can simply put you onto the street on the day the fixed term expires – there are legal processes that need to be used to evict *any* assured shorthold tenant. However it does mean that, once these fixed terms come to an end, any landlord has a legal right to insist on having their property vacated (this legal process is explained in Lesson 12). Control of how long you remain reverts absolutely to your landlord once your fixed term ends and that decision will almost always depend on your conduct as a tenant. However, they don't need *any legal reason whatever* to ask you to leave after that.

During your initial fixed term, you do enjoy a degree of security – in other words, you'd have to be breaching a significant element(s) of your lease – like not paying rent or causing damage – before any court would agree to terminate your contract during the initial, relatively secure, fixed term. In return for this limited security, you become liable for rent during the **entire fixed term**. The longer the fixed term, the longer your security *and* your liability for the rent (with some safeguards, explained later).

## Where to start your searching

### Online research

www.whatever is an excellent place to search through, but online letting has not yet really taken off. Although it's an invaluable research tool, most private landlords (who remain the majority providers) still stick with newspaper advertisements. This means that online alone can actually distort your view to the only set of suppliers who always use it i.e. the letting agents, whose rents are often higher because they incorporate fees. Make sure you never rely on only one perspective in such a diverse marketplace. Even if you're searching from some distant town (or country) make sure that you explore all the options.

### Specialist services

■ Students should always explore their own university's accommodation service where decent property is often available. Check whether or not these units have been checked for safety – some universities simply provide lists, others carry out extensive safety checks and accredit property.

■ Other tenants may wish to try contacting the local authority in the area they're looking to rent in – many grew so tired of substandard accommodation that they drew up lists of accredited properties that comply with all safety requirements and have responsible landlords. Quite a few now have extensive lists of recommended properties that rarely come onto the open market via agents or the newspapers.

■ Both the above options are a great place to start for students and the second is an excellent first choice for all tenants looking for keenly priced units.

■ Tenants searching for property whose first consideration is not cost but location could do worse than explore a local relocation service – however once found, the terms/conditions would not be 'guaranteed' and users still need to read the full guide to avoid pitfalls.

### The lettings agencies

Most towns are now awash with lettings agencies. These companies are keenly commercial operations which exist to make profits, not to be your friends, no matter how much of a welcome mat they put out for you. They are employed by landlords, not tenants – renting through an agency does not make *you* their customer, they already have their client – landlords. A quick walk down any high street, or a brief scan through any local paper will show you just how many there are. Every one of them has property on their books and is actively looking to get tenants into contracts. But *beware:* all agents have *many* additional up front fees. Added up, they can come as quite a shock to the unwary.

**WARNING ANECDOTE**

Agents are forbidden by law from charging tenants for simply providing lists of available accommodation. Stories are emerging however that some London agencies are trying to charge a fee *to show* you a property. If someone asks you for seventy-five pounds to even view a flat ... do yourself a favour, find another agency.

Finding accommodation through agents can have some unexpectedly high add-on costs and I take a look at some likely ones in Lesson 5. These can add up to significant sums of money simply to get to the contract stage so make sure that you check the agency lesson carefully – especially if you're on a tight budget.

### Independent landlords

Like agents, landlords exist to make profits. They are often also landlords who prefer more direct relationships with their lettings – especially over tenant selection. However, because their costs are reduced by not paying agency fees, many offer slightly lower rents. In addition, few make charges for basic tenancy set-up services. They usually look on the **inventory** processes at both ends of the contract as part and parcel of setting up a well organised tenancy. Nor do many independents charge **lease signing fees**, **extension fees** or any of the other variations dreamed up by agencies. Many don't charge **check in, check out fees** or **inventory** costs either.

### Checking your options

You pays your money and you takes your choice in the rental game. So always at least *examine* your options beyond the easy high street strategy. If ever a market thrived on choice it's the huge lettings market. Checking out your options can save you a great deal of money over the lifetime of a rental contract.

## A word about the paperwork

All sensible private landlords/agents do require their younger tenants (students and the under 25s usually) to provide a **Parental Guarantor**. Effectively what this means is that all the responsibilities like rent, bills and especially damage are underwritten or 'guaranteed' by someone older who is presumed to be more responsible than the young tenant (and to have more cash!).

---

**WARNING ANECDOTE**

A responsible landlord, having just refurbished a whole house, rented it at 8 p.m. to three young people. When he returned the next morning, as arranged, to do one final job in the new kitchen, he found that the contents of the coffee machine had been tipped into the centre of the new lounge carpet, and five cigarette ends had been stubbed out and left in the centre of the coffee. They had been in place less than 12 hours and had caused over £400 worth of damage!

So, landlords do need these guarantees. Sometimes people moving out of home for the first time simply don't get to grips with the realities of costs and care for property that all tenants contractually agree to when signing leases, or other rather basic bits of knowledge either.

### WARNING ANECDOTE

A young, unemployed man took a flat. His mother clearly wanted him to leave home, and paid the deposit; she also happily signed a parental guarantor form for the agent. Her son moved in, and within a week the two tenants downstairs contacted the agent. Hot purple water was pouring through their bedroom ceiling. An emergency plumber was sent to investigate. The young home leaver had acquired an automatic washing machine, and had fitted it himself. The plumber looked, and asked where the waste pipe had been fitted.

'What waste pipe?' he replied innocently.

'Perhaps the one still fitted snugly with plastic ties to the base of the machine?' the plumber suggested.

Gallons of hot soapy water had run through the building that week.

The agent decided to visit and have firm words with the tenant. When the lad opened the door, a big footed Rottweiler puppy jumped up to greet him. Another impulse purchase? When contacted the mother simply had no idea of the implication of the guarantee she had so recently signed, and would be held to by a rightly efficient agent.

'But surely you can claim on the insurance?' was her response. A full repair account was sent to the mother.

### Tenants' application procedure

Many landlords/agents will also want to instigate a **tenants' application procedure** of some sort – another form where tenants are
legally obliged to reveal information like former addresses, their
National Insurance Number (or passport number) and a variety of
other verifying personal details. They will almost always require
authorisation for **credit checks**. This kind of paperwork is essential
for landlords (or their agents). Make sure you fill in details truthfully.
These documents are fast becoming adopted by most landlords and
agents.

### Ground 17

Since 1997 one of the grounds upon which tenants can be asked to
leave (even during the relatively safe fixed term) is **Ground 17**, and
the period of notice of your landlord's intention to seek possession in
this case can be as little as two weeks (see Lesson 11 for further details
on grounds for possession).

Ground 17 allows landlords to act if they were persuaded or induced
to grant the tenancy as a result of a false statement, knowingly made
by the tenant, or someone acting at the tenant's instigation. This was
a very significant addition to the rights of possession your landlord had
before 1997, and a necessary one. Tenants who now claim to be
employed when they are not, for example, could be affected. So too
could tenants who pretend to be older than they in fact are, where
landlords have age restrictions. Students have often failed to admit that
they are students because many landlords do indeed avoid them.
Application forms are a protection for landlords and agents against any
such false statement.

This Ground enables landlords who have been told untruths to use
that as a legal reason for the prompt return of their property. **Tenancy
application forms** are a useful way therefore of making sure that
landlords and agencies have written proof of the tenants' claims.
Prospective tenants would be well advised to remember this when
filling them in.

### Other types of guarantee

Sometimes tenants have circumstances which require specialist guarantees. An excellent example of this is for the tenant who wants to move in, say, with the family dog. Most leases specifically exclude pets, but if you need a home with your dog, and you discuss it in advance, many agents and landlords will agree. They do however normally expect you to provide additional levels of deposit against damage, and often ask you to sign a guarantee that you will replace to their satisfaction any items (including garden lawns) that have been damaged. They also usually demand additional end-of-lease cleaning.

But the majority, i.e. honest tenants, shouldn't fear the paperwork. It's part and parcel of getting off on the right foot, of giving your landlord the confidence to let you rent what is a very expensive asset for a tiny part of its value each month. It's healthy having exactly what both parties agreed set out in writing, and it protects both the landlord *and* the tenant. Landlords/agents who are organised enough to have procedures like this are also the ones most likely to respond to genuine problems like repairs because they're set up to make their contracts run smoothly, hence protecting their own vital income stream.

### Beware the absence of paperwork

Avoid like the plague the landlord willing to offer some 'back of the envelope' type of tenancy – the last thing a modern tenant needs is a landlord who skirts round the legalities over such huge financial obligations. Organised landlords know what they need. They're the ones who aren't interested in scams, in trying to charge for things that have never been discussed, let alone agreed to by tenants. Okay, in reality an assured shorthold tenancy can be legally set up without a shred of paperwork – but that's *not* what you want. Organisation proves a mindset of responsibility and with rents this high, who wants a disorganised landlord when the boiler breaks down? Or all those fights over what the conditions were when deposits need returning? Paperwork protects tenants and landlords. Don't be tempted to skirt round them in such costly contracts. It's a recipe for future trouble.

### A word about inventory costs

Let's be clear here, whether you're renting from a private landlord or via an agent, inventories are absolutely essential to protect both tenants and landlords. You need an inventory – a freshly prepared one that accurately reflects the genuine condition of the property.

Inventories are closely tied into the **deposit** structure – so they really *do* matter and are explained more fully in Lesson 4.

> Tenants agreeing to take on a property that doesn't come with a brand new, up-to-date inventory, which they've checked through, agreed and signed as an accurate record of condition, are asking for trouble when they move out. Consider yourselves warned. Accommodation without paperwork is a sure sign of careless management (landlord or agent) – and that's the *last* thing you want to be paying a small fortune for.

Inventories are one of the most contentious areas of 'the business' and so closely tied into the deposit structure that no sensible tenant can afford to be blasé about them. Read up on deposit charges and inventories – not knowing what you're legally liable for can be a very costly bit of ignorance.

## Examining the options realistically

All these various charges and services need to be considered when working out what you can and cannot afford. Tenants renting relatively lower priced units very often find themselves renting via independent landlords who simply don't generate the profit levels needed to engage agents – or choose not to pay them because they know perfectly well how to run a tenancy. Also bear in mind that agency fees for many other services can be very hefty. Not only do they levy high fees from the landlord for their services, but also their end of lease redecorating, cleaning, and repair services can be very expensive – especially if they have a good sized deposit to work through at the end of a tenancy. (Much of this will thankfully change with the new **Tenancy Deposit Scheme** – explained later – soon to come on-stream.)

Sometimes properties available to let through agencies can be more expensive than similar properties available direct from private landlords. The landlord's agency fees have to be incorporated within the rent, and *you* will be paying them. Agencies usually charge landlords around 15 per cent plus VAT of the rent for management – money that comes from higher rents. For some tenants this is worthwhile, but many others prefer to find their own landlord.

## Finding the independent landlord

Check the local classified section or 'property to let' column. Many of the advertisements will have been placed by agents, but they are often required to indicate that they are trade, or to state their company. Some free advertising papers even require anything other than private advertising to be in bold print so that it is very easy to recognise. Rule of thumb. Wherever it's glitzy, it's an agent.

Look through the smaller adverts and there you'll find thousands of private landlords who advertise here direct – every single day of the week. Check the price range you are looking for. Rental valuations depend on a number of different factors; the area, the condition and the facilities offered. The valuations will vary, so check over a couple of weeks to get a feel for the price range you are looking for before you start making appointments to view. And again, watch out for charlatans.

---

**WARNING ANECDOTE**

Bargains are usually too good to be true. One canny landlord was recently discovered to be showing tenants a rather fancy property at what seemed a very cheap rent. For consideration, he demanded an up front fee for referencing, which came to several hundred pounds for each viewer – and at such a bargain basement price he got a great deal of interest. All applicants were rejected on the grounds of unsatisfactory references – many lost hundreds of pounds each. This case is being investigated by Trading Standards, but illustrates perfectly that there's always someone with a well worked scam just around the corner. Always beware someone asking for huge upfront sums of *your* money.

### A cautionary word

Renting property through well run agencies can have some unrecognised benefits. Some agencies (but by no means a majority yet) are members of trade associations that monitor standards and they should check basic safety provision on furniture, gas safety, etc of anything on their books because they have legal liabilities themselves if they don't. This doesn't apply to independent landlords, where tenants need to proactively check basic safety for themselves. And, unfortunately, the worst landlords of all, offering the dangerous property, can't get taken onto the books of any legitimate agent, meaning they always advertise in the press along with the overwhelming majority of responsible landlords. Be very wary of any property that seems clearly cheaper (or tackier) than its competitors. Safety isn't something you can *afford* to be casual about. See Lesson 2 on viewings for advice.

## Things you need to know

### Deposits

There's much more information on this topic in a later lesson, but as a rule of thumb, most agents/private landlords will want at least a month's rent to hold against damages. Many will ask for the equivalent of six weeks' rent. This should be held for you (and always remains your money) until the end of the tenancy. This is a big topic and one about which you'll find a whole lesson later in the guide.

### Advance rent

All landlords and their agents expect tenants to pay for their accommodation in advance. Usually the required amount is a month (or four weeks' rent) and rent needs to stay in advance at all times to satisfy your lease.

### How is it valued?

The biggest inclusion of all here is location, which can add or subtract huge sums to or from the rent. It's a simple fact that there is now property right across the range and to suit all pockets. The less you have to spend, the further you'll walk to the shops. Know what you are looking for, and where you can afford, because careless mistakes can haunt you in the lettings game.

### What's included in the rent

Rent is just that – unless it specifically provides for inclusions (which should be clearly stated). Rent does *not* include council tax, water rates or TV licence and it certainly won't usually include electricity or gas costs.

### Facilities

When trying to work out what seems a reasonable rent, take into account what *is* being included. And make sure that you learn the shorthand. P/F means part furnished; C/H means central heating; S/C means self contained.

### U/F

Unfurnished accommodation is for the serious renter and provides nothing but the building, facilities (kitchen/bathroom) and a heating system. It may include carpets. It is expensive to equip and, unless you have a number of personal possessions, this is probably not for you. Unfurnished is also a real rarity – there are historic reasons for this that I won't bore you with. If renting U/F look for a long initial 'fixed term' – it simply isn't cost effective to move in and out of this type of unit twice a year.

### P/F

Many, many properties are offered part-furnished (P/F), which usually means carpets, curtains, cooker, fridge. Some landlords and many agents prefer it because there are strict requirements on the safety of supplied beds, sofas, etc in furnished units (which will be detailed later in Lesson 2). Again, it takes a great deal of money to equip these units and the P/F rent can often look attractive because less is being offered. That can make P/F much less cost effective in the long run, whereas fully furnished (F/F) will cost a little more. Always make sure you that are comparing like with like when doing your research.

### F/F

F/F means fully furnished and should include all furniture, carpets, beds, curtains, etc that you need to live comfortably, but won't usually include items like crockery, bed linen and small kitchen appliances like kettles and toasters. This is by far the most common type of rental. It's a hugely popular arrangement and the most widely offered because moving in and out is cheap and yet tenants can 'personalise' a bit.

### Note

If you choose to take a furnished unit, and then want it unfurnished so that you can take your own furniture, it can actually cost you *more,* because you will have to pay for removal and storage of your landlord's belongings. Check the cost implications of this before you arrange it.

### F/F eqpt

Rarely, properties come fully furnished and fully equipped (F/F/eqpt) and these should have everything you need (furniture, crockery, and sometimes even linen – everything *including* the kitchen sink!).

> Tenants taking fully furnished and equipped accommodation need not only an excellent inventory, they also need to live very carefully. One broken plate, which could have been part of a set, and full replacement of a complete new matching set could quite reasonably be required by the landlord or agent.

Any tenant considering taking on a high spec unit where every item is provided should seriously consider engaging an independent inventory service – easily found in any *Yellow Pages*. Private landlords will usually (but not always!) split the costs with you as this is of shared benefit. You simply have no idea how much hassle two sensible people can create over a single broken wine glass. Get it in writing!

---

**WARNING ANECDOTE**

Don't think that the very rich don't rent. They do. And landlords offering very high spec units are expected to make very certain that their goods are in order. One wealthy tenant successfully sued a landlord because a wonky leg on the antique dining table resulted in an accident involving the tenant's own costly china and a ruined dinner party.

## What should you pay?

Obviously, the more you are being offered, the higher the rent will be. But don't try to economise on what you need. It isn't much of an economy to rent part-furnished and then have to spend a fortune buying beds and sofas. After all, most tenants do not actually own a houseful of furniture. Never take a property without real thought which doesn't come complete with carpets. Only the very rash would seriously consider carpeting a house or flat on the basis of six months' guaranteed security.

### How the rent can be calculated

Whoever you choose to rent from, watch how the rent is actually calculated. If the property is advertised as a rent 'pcm' (per calendar month) you will make 12 monthly payments in any one year. If the rent is weekly, you will make 52 weekly payments in any year. This can actually make quite a considerable difference – many landlords have 13 lots of four weeks in their years!

Check it this way. If you are being quoted a weekly rent, multiply it by 52, then divide that total by 12 to check out the calendar month costs. The rent on what actually sounds cheaper could in fact be quite a fair bit higher, and most experienced landlords and many long-standing agencies do not use pcm rents for this very reason. It's the basic retail £1.99 rather than £2.00 strategy. Most agencies on the other hand do prefer pcm rents because it makes their monthly accounting process easier. Plus people who are paid on a pcm basis can sometimes prefer it too.

> Rent £100 per week × 52 = total annual cost £5,200 per year
> Rent £400 pcm × 12 = total annual cost £4,800 per year

As this very clearly shows, there can be a difference of £400 per year between these rents due to the thirteenth month. Yet to the inexperienced, they can sound broadly the same.

### A word about negotiation

Prospective tenants are often advised to negotiate over rent. This can be much easier to say than to do. Most landlords/agents will not even consider price negotiations. Some will. It will depend absolutely on market conditions and how they are affecting supply at the time. Only you can be the judge of that from your basic research. If dozens of two-bed flats within a mile are constantly advertising, it may be worth a shot.

However, in a market where good, or even half decent mid-range property is going fast, the reality is that your attempted negotiations may not be appreciated. Many landlords are actually pretty uncomfortable about attempts at negotiation. They may even take it personally; feel that you are trying to 'knock down' a property they think is delightful. Try it by all means, but don't be especially surprised if you're shown the door.

One genuine exception to this advice is for the cash-rich tenant (admittedly a bit of a rarity). If you're in a position to pay your rent for several months in advance, this provides an excellent negotiating opportunity. Landlords who can't see the benefit in this arrangement are rarer than cash-rich tenants. For the majority, it is unfortunately a matter of looking around carefully for the best available unit, and paying, except in unusual circumstances, the rent asked for.

### For students

Those of you lucky enough to have money in the bank at the beginning of term may well be able to secure property not usually let to students by offering to pay 'upfront'. It may be painful, but it can really help secure a better unit from a more nervous landlord.

## Choosing a property

### If you decide to find property through the classifieds

You need to be organised before you pick up the phone. You need a pen and paper, and a list of sensible questions will save you time and disappointments (suggestions are given later in this Lesson). Any responsible landlord will be more than happy to discuss these with you before you traipse miles for a viewing. It can be really frustrating trying to get information on the phone, but persevere.

If the private landlord you are trying to reach is permanently unavailable, or their partner doesn't know the answer to any of your questions, or indeed if the landlord simply cannot be bothered to chat to you on the phone for a few minutes, ask yourself how interested they'll be when the boiler breaks down in January. Find a helpful, *organised* landlord who sounds as if they know what they're doing.

### The real decision is yours

It can often seem much easier on balance to use an agency than to start ringing around the classifieds. Others of you will either not be willing or able to afford the kind of charges that agents routinely levy on tenants. Each tenant must balance the factors and whether or not they can afford an extra few hundred pounds that agencies charge to set up a tenancy, whereas with a private landlord those costs should be minimal.

In addition you must decide whether or not you would prefer to know, and have direct access to, your own landlord, or whether you would be happier dealing through a third party. Not everyone finds the same circumstances comfortable. However, if the agency you called for details doesn't get around to sending them, or hasn't the time to discuss a big revenue earner like this on the phone, ask yourself again, just how reliable are *they* likely to be when that boiler breaks down in January? Find another agency.

### The only guarantee in this business

I can confidently guarantee that any conscientious landlord or agent will be responsive and helpful from the outset. If you are having difficulty communicating *before* you sign the contract, things are unlikely to improve once you have done so.

### Some sensible questions to ask before you make an appointment to view any property

- How much is the rent?
- What, if anything, does it include?
- Is it payable weekly or monthly?
- How much deposit is required?
- How much rent is required in advance?

■ How is this to be paid – cash, cheque, banker's draft?
■ Are references/credit references required?
■ How much will these cost each?
■ What is included in the rent – e.g. is there a washing machine (include what you need).
■ How much are the water rates and council tax per month?
■ How is the property heated?
■ Is there an inventory charge, and/or a vacating check charge?
■ What are you responsible for – gardens, hallway cleaning, etc?

## Please note

If you do make an appointment to view, either keep it or cancel it. Don't just leave landlords standing outside a property waiting for you to turn up. It is unfair, discourteous and regrettably very common. Personally, I won't now go to any arranged viewing unless the prospective tenant rings an hour before to confirm that they still intend turning up – and I never wait longer than 15 minutes.

# Lesson 2

# Viewings

## What to look for

After your research and questions, you should eventually have a list of several properties that you have made appointments to view, through agents, landlords or a combination. The advice I'm giving you here has to be general. You'll need to apply it to a wide variety of buildings and situations by using that most vital tool for renters – your common sense. However, as you go through a property, you *need* to be on the lookout for safety issues, which is why I have included them in this section.

You should have appointments to view with either private landlords, or agency staff, and you still need to find out quite a lot from whoever you're meeting before you rush to sign on that dotted line. You are looking for a property that suits your needs, is within your budget and is *safe*. A viewing is your first (and possibly only) chance to learn almost all you'll need to know about 'the deal' on offer. It should be a two-way process, where both landlord/agent and tenant discuss matters and decide whether or not they want to do business with each other. Don't agree to accept a property if the agency sends you round with a viewer who doesn't have a clue how to answer your questions. If that happens, note down your queries and go back to the agency looking for answers *before* you agree to sign contracts.

Avoid landlords who won't talk to you – if they're unwilling to explain anything now, things are unlikely to improve after you've agreed to hand over all that money.

## What to avoid

No matter how tight your budget though, you must find somewhere safe to live. At the bottom end of the market, this is not as easy as it ought to be. And don't assume expensive means safe either.

**WARNING ANECDOTE**

A consultancy at a prestigious lettings agency lasted less than four hours for me. When I asked where the gas safety certificates and electrical certifications were kept, I was looked at in astonishment. Almost 300 lets – many at thousands of pounds per week – and not a single gas safety or electrical inspection certificate between the lot of them. The owner of the agency thought these regulations were for poor people's homes. Always ask to see gas safety certificates, they're a clear sign of competent management.

Many properties, especially at the lower end of the price range and often let to young sharers, are still technically unsafe, or unfit to live in (new rules about this were introduced in the Housing Act 2004 and came into force July 2007 – check Lesson 14 on Houses in Multiple Occupation if you're a sharer). Although regulations exist to protect tenants they are monitored by overburdened local authorities, who, despite their best efforts, often do not even realise that a particular property is being let out at all.

There are still a significant minority of landlords who operate quite outside the law, and who continue to offer dreadfully inadequate property to tenants but who've happily hoiked their rent to near market norms. However, simply reading a guide doesn't really give a flavour of either the state, smell nor overall levels of dilapidation that confront some tenants as they walk into some properties.

> Welcome to the world of tenants on tight budgets.

This chapter will try to give you some overall pointers on what to check for, whatever the price range. Decent landlords/agents will offer property that is clean and *reasonably* presented (which doesn't mean expensively decked out). Expect that as a basic demand.

> There is always something better to be found – even for the most *s-t-r-e-t-c-h-e-d* tenants – than a dangerous dump.

# Advice about viewings

Before we begin considering specifics, the very best advice you can take is never to view alone. It is simply not wise to make appointments to go into empty properties with *anyone* you have never met before.

Besides which, there is simply too much to take in. It can be very difficult to remember everything you'll need to, particularly if you're viewing numerous properties over several days. Take a pad and pen and make notes – no one will mind a bit. If you are looking to share with other tenants, make sure that you're all available to view together. Landlords and agents can quite reasonably be reluctant to reshow one property to various members of a group at different times.

### The holding deposit

Be prepared for a request for a **holding deposit** if you do like and want a property (so long as you're satisfied that all your questions have been answered. If not, hold onto your money until they have been). Holding deposits are a sum of money (usually about a week's rent) that tenants hand over fairly soon after viewings to prove good intent – in other words, that they seriously want to rent a unit. This money may be used to fund references/credit checks – or it may not. This is something that you need to pin down. Find out exactly what you're paying out for. It's amazing, for example, just how much of this can disappear in costs when using agents with multiple reference charges.

### Get a receipt

Make sure you ask for receipts for all holding deposits and indeed for full rental deposits too. These receipts should state exactly what the money is for, what costs you agree to be deducted from it and what circumstances will trigger a full refund. *Then keep them safe.*

Don't imagine that, having agreed to take a property and having handed over a holding deposit, your brand new prospective landlord won't continue showing it to other potential tenants. Similarly, most agencies will continue viewings until all the references you have provided are found to be acceptable. The paperwork required to establish tenancies isn't instantaneous and most landlords/agents will hedge their bets until a much closer contractual stage has been reached.

Always remember that until all the necessary leases have been signed, and full monies exchanged, *no contract exists at all.*

### If your references don't stack up

Tenants who have paid part deposits may lose significant sums for referencing and administration if their prospective landlord/agent quite reasonably rejects them because references were poor or credit checks shaky. Keep an eye on your credit history – having a poor one can be an expensive mistake for prospective tenants.

If, however, you have paid a holding or full deposit out and you still want the property, then a private landlord/agent subsequently lets to someone else whom they simply *prefer*, you should expect a full refund.

### Getting your ducks in a row

When you *really* want a particular property, you need to ensure that the paperwork required by your landlord/agent is quickly made available, and that you have the money required ready and waiting. Do not expect anyone to hold a property for you for days or weeks, while you sort yourself out. It simply won't happen.

### Learn how to say 'no'

If, on the other hand you don't want a unit, say so. It's quite amazing how many tenants are too embarrassed to say 'no thank you' to landlords and agents. If you definitely don't want it, say so. If you're undecided, say so. Landlords and agents are quite used to hearing 'No thanks, this one's not for me.'

## How to start looking

Learning how to choose a good rental involves quite a bit of thinking on your feet. If you are lucky enough to be able to visit the area and look at the properties from the outside before you have your viewing, so much the better. This is often an excellent way of screening out those properties you simply don't want before you go inside. However, if your viewing is the first opportunity you have to look at the property, look around carefully.

- Does it look neglected?
- Is it in noticeably worse condition than its neighbours?
- Is the area worse than the flat you saw yesterday for much the same rent?

If you are about to pay average or above average rent for the area, and the answer to these questions is yes, then decline, and move on to your next viewing. However, if you are struggling to find something that you can afford, you'll probably have less choice. Unless shocked, continue your inspection – you're now looking for basic safety – gas safety certificates, fire resistant labels on sofas – safety is the one thing that no tenant should economise on – but that doesn't stop unsafe buildings being commonplace. There are very heavy fines for land-lords/agents caught letting out property with dangerous facilities.

Remember that landlords/agents willing to take such serious financial risks are unlikely to make reliable parties to much else in a contract. The poisonous relationship of bad landlord working in conjunction with some less scrupulous agents often works in tandem to keep poor property circulating on the rental market. This type of deliberate flouting costs lives every year.

> Take your safety *seriously* and don't pay out good money to become another tragic statistic.

### *Don't be rushed through viewings*

Whether your budget is modest or huge, don't feel obliged to rush through any viewing in five minutes. It is a very common problem. Looking at watches, talking about their next appointment – none of this is your problem. You are here to examine the contents and conditions of a very expensive contract. Ignore the pressure to rush.

Always remember that all landlords/agents need tenants as much as you need a place to rent. This is a very competitive market these days and no one is running a charity here. You don't need hours to view a place, but don't allow yourself to be hurried through in a few minutes either. Nor to be prevented from asking some basic questions. You, or your group, will be paying thousands of pounds to rent any property for a single year, plus you will be contractually bound in most cases for at least six months – in other words, stuck with it. Be wary of landlords/agents who can't give you a bit of time to look round and answer a few basic questions.

### Being businesslike

Obviously the higher your budget, the higher your expectations should be. Don't be afraid to try asking for, say, a new carpet to seal the deal – and get any agreements in *writing*. Landlords operating in areas where gluts of properties clog up the market can be surprisingly co-operative. Empty units are hardly a landlord's ideal scenario – every empty day costs them money. Besides, remember – this is a *business* transaction. Be businesslike! Landlords aren't always looking for people who haven't a clue what they're doing. Believe me, rental virgins can be very hard work.

Finally, never feel pressured to make an instant decision.

> *Always ask for an inventory to be drawn up.* Sound as if you know what you're doing and you're likely to get less sharp practice.

Beyond that, you can always go away and think about it for a short while. A quick dose of caffeine can often be all it takes to help you decide yes or no.

### Feeling that 'comfort factor'

Make sure that you are comfortable enough with your chosen landlord and be sure you ask who to report serious faults or the ubiquitous 'lost keys' to – and preferably get a landline phone number. A good question to ask is how long a serious fault would take to be repaired. Landlords who struggle to answer or who seem put out that you've asked should be given a wide berth if possible. And that 'mobile only' landlord can be hard to track down when the roof leaks.

Similarly with agents – though you can never be their customer – find an agent who is pleasant to deal with, who responds as promised and doesn't break their word. These things matter in long business relationships. And again, don't assume anything. Ask how long major repairs usually take and ask who to call on Christmas Day if the roof leaks. Most decent sized agents have a 24-hour emergency service.

## What am I looking for?

### Keep your eyes open

Look for:

- units where someone has cleaned up
- where kitchen units seems sturdy and carpets are well fixed down as a bare minimum
- fridges and cookers need to be clean and to work.

Open fridge doors, switch on a cooker knob – it only takes a minute. Ask about appliances – are they covered by service contracts in case of breakdown? Tie up these details exactly. If washing machines, dishwashers, etc are included in the rent then it is the landlord's responsibility to keep them working. Except... and there always is one... if you damage the item. So, if the pump fails in a washing machine, the landlord should pay for a repair. If however, you have clogged up the filter with hairpins, expect a repair bill. This is a good rule of thumb. If anything (sinks, drains, etc) was in good working order when you moved in and your lifestyle has caused a problem, you will be charged for repairs.

### Gas appliances

Without any exceptions at all, every landlord or agent *must* make sure that *every* gas appliance has a *current* gas safety certificate. Lots of tenants are either too embarrassed, or too nervous of being shown the door to check for essential safety requirements. They shouldn't be, but in the real world tenants often feel quite intimidated, especially if they are inexperienced. If you are worried about asking for certificates, a more subtle approach may well work. Casually ask how long it is since, say, the gas boiler/fire was serviced. Any responsible landlord or agent will be prompted to tell you about the annual safety check.

If no information is volunteered, you really need to follow this up. Do you really want this flat enough to be slowly poisoned by carbon monoxide? One notorious carbon monoxide poisoning incident is too sensitive to be included here – even as an anecdote. Every landlord and some agents are liable to massive fines for ignoring this legislation. You seriously have to ask yourself – if your potential new landlord is willing to take that risk, what else is s/he prepared to risk, while they live in some nice safe house elsewhere?

### WARNING ANECDOTE

This author recently heard the following tale from a student in the north of England. The gas fire in a student house did not work properly. Repeated calls to the landlord were ignored, and the tenants eventually called out a major gas company to look at the fire. The engineer declared the fire dangerous, but the tenants could not afford the repair. The engineer placed a sticker on the fire stating that the appliance was dangerous and told them *not* to use it. It was May, and they managed without the heating. Weeks later, the landlord was showing around prospective tenants for the next academic year. He ripped off the sticker, and told the tenants that if they warned the new tenants about the dangerous fire, he wouldn't return a penny of their deposits!

Such conduct is hugely intimidating. If your landlord or agency doesn't make all the gas appliances safe, do us all a favour and report them to the Environmental Health Department of your local council. These people work hard to ensure tenants are safe – they'll be interested in unsafe practices, believe me.

## Furnishings

Landlords/agents who let out property which is furnished are *responsible* under various laws to make sure that everything provided is safe. All upholstered furniture must comply with British Standards. This will usually mean that on beds, sofas, cushions (anything upholstered basically) you should find a triangular label with a BS trademark attached. However, the easiest way of recognising what you're looking for is to pop into any furniture showroom and have a look at a label before you start looking at units for rent. If you can't find any safety label on the furniture in the unit you're viewing, ask yourself why not. If the landlord claims that the label fell off (well it can happen) – simply lift up the upholstered seats, compliant furniture will have further labels stitched firmly onto the seat/frame.

> Again, don't take a property where the landlord is prepared to ignore this widely publicised rule. Who knows what else might not be safe? Responsible landlords don't provide dangerous furniture, and who wants an irresponsible landlord?

If the property is part-furnished it is simpler to examine because there is less to check. Check that the carpets, curtains, etc are in reasonable condition. Part-furnished properties should also have 'white goods', cooker, fridge, perhaps a dishwasher. Check that they work. Ask whom to contact if there is a problem, and how quickly repairs are usually made.

Unfurnished properties are perhaps the simplest of all – nothing to check for but doors, walls, windows, and a roof! Do check though that cooker points and plumbing for washing machines/dishwashers, etc are in place. You will also need a current gas safety certificate for any gas boiler.

> If you're not convinced that the facilities are safe, look elsewhere. You might even feel confident enough to let the landlord know why you're not interested. If landlords repeatedly find their property rejected on safety grounds, they'll perhaps see the wisdom in complying with the law. We really *cannot* expect trading standards or environmental health officers to find every problem, there simply aren't enough of them and many landlords let out buildings on the 'quiet'. Tenants need to be proactive if standards are to be raised. Lettings has always attracted an unattractive rump of individuals who want a nice income stream that no one knows about. Don't expect integrity, expect safety labels.

## A tip

Every single conscientious landlord I have ever met provides smoke alarms, hand held fire extinguishers and fire blankets in kitchens as a basic. They do so to protect both their tenants and their investments. Look for that mindset in your prospective landlord.

## Electricity

Landlords/agents are also expected to ensure that the electrical wiring, and any electrical appliances which *they* provide, are safe. Unfortunately, this definition of 'safe' is rather open, in a way that certification for gas appliances is not. Private landlords are advised to have their electrical supply checked by a certified electrician every two years, but currently this is an advisory rather than compulsory requirement in most 'standard' rentals.

Tenants must therefore exercise common sense. It is not being seriously suggested that you bring in an electrician, but do look out for obvious problems as you do your viewing. Loose sockets, or too few, with numerous adaptors might concern you. Sockets in silly or unexpected places, such as really near the sink, or in a bathroom, might ring a warning bell. Single sockets can indicate an old-fashioned system. Round-pin sockets are definite ones to avoid. Good signs would be:

- An adequate supply of well fitted sockets, fitted *above* rather than inserted into skirting boards.

- Clean, white (rather than yellowing or brown) electrical cable to light fittings.

- A circuit breaker system and modern fuse box where simple switching replaces old fashioned fuse wire are also excellent things to come across in rentals.

Free-standing electric fires are something definitely to avoid. If appliances are included, check for worn wiring or loose plugs. There's a real difference between the elderly electrical system that a home owner may be willing to accept and that which a landlord must provide. The difference is brutal – it's called money. Live how you like as individuals, but the minute you begin charging other people to live in buildings, expect the safety bar to be raised.

## Note

There are very particular, more stringent requirements relating to electrical wiring and facilities in Houses in Multiple Occupation. If this is the type of accommodation you're looking for, please take the time to read Lesson 14.

> Not everyone can rent top-notch property with every single gizmo in place. Yet the vast majority of rentals are safe and have happy tenants, unless they are used carelessly by tenants themselves. One landlord I know is currently rebuilding an entire three bedroom house, burned down when tenants left their laundry to dry on perfectly safe storage heaters once too often when they left for the pub.

## Safety issues

In cheaper properties some rogue landlords can cover up old wiring systems with shiny new switches and sockets. A brief look, say in the cupboard under the stairs, can often readily reveal old rubber wiring and a 30-year old fuse box. Here the value of taking someone else with you to view can really pay dividends. While you innocently talk to the landlord about the garden, your dad or your friend could be having a peek at the electrics under the stairs near the meter. If you're viewing with a reputable agency, no subterfuge is necessary. Ask when the last electrical check was carried out. They should have a note on file.

### WARNING ANECDOTES

I visited a student house in London. Old, brown, cloth-covered wiring hung down to every light fitting. Many of the sockets were round pin. The landlord had augmented this already deficient supply by stringing long lengths of wire *from the lighting sockets* to which numerous long block adaptors were attached. Admittedly, in a house with old furniture covered in brown nylon fabric, with suppurating bursts of foam guaranteed to suffocate everyone in the event of a (highly likely) fire, one would not really have expected a recent wiring report. This landlord's only concession to modern standards was his realisation that most of us don't have stereos/computers with round-pin plugs. Oh, and there were cockroaches. Yuk, yuk. A swift call to the local Environmental Health Department soon closed this landlord down.

Other students were offered a flat with a washing machine in the bathroom, right next to the bath. When challenged about how safe this was, the agent insisted the bathroom was not a bathroom at all, but a *washroom* (which presumably just happened to have a bath, washbasin and toilet in it). Now, before you think that the washing machine might have been a welcome additional resource, just imagine the potential consequences of deciding to switch off the machine, while *you* were submerged in a deep, relaxing bath.

Tenants really have to learn how to look out for their own safety. Remember that most rented property is never even seen by a member of any authority. Some landlords rent out dangerous units. And some agencies aren't too scrupulous about what they take on their books. Look out for yourself! In the world of lettings there are no guarantees and believe what you see, not what you assume.

## General condition

Having looked at the features, you will also need to take in the general condition of the property. Do try to avoid, if financially feasible, properties in obvious states of disrepair. Property ought to look fresh, clean and the contents be in reasonable condition. Again, the higher the rent, the higher you have every right to pitch your expectations. Presentation right across the price range can be some of the most obvious evidence about the *quality* of the management.

Smart, clean looking units (from the cheapest to the finest) will tend to have efficient management, efficient repair systems, good inventories and management systems. Neglected property is owned or being run by someone who doesn't care. This 'run on the back of an envelope' type of management is not usually very responsive when you need something repaired either, so try to find something better if you can.

However, sometimes appearances can be deceptive. It's amazing just what you can cover with a can of paint.

**WARNING ANECDOTE**

Four tenants took a small, apparently pleasant terraced house during their second year at university. The bedrooms were freshly decorated, and everything looked fine. However, it soon became obvious that chronic damp was affecting one of the main walls. The landlord did eventually arrange for work to be done. Unfortunately, that work involved removing *all* the internal plaster. The external repairs were never completed, the inside never replastered, and the tenant had little alternative but to sleep in a soaking room for two cold terms. To add final insult to injury, the landlord deducted the cost of redecoration from the tenants' deposit...as there were some finger marks on the wall! A sharp phone call from one of the parents soon sorted this guy out – but not everyone has clued up parents.

The lettings industry is bedevilled with stories like this, and it is very hard for people who haven't been tenants to really believe what can and does go on. The student market and the market for young people can be especially tough. For most people, the upheaval of finding somewhere else, and getting a deposit returned in time to move on can be so difficult that they have no choice but to suffer bad housing. Tenants who have looked quite carefully do have at least a chance to pick up on potential problems before they sign up.

### For singletons and couples (new safety rules)

Many tenancies are individual or, at most taken on in pairs. However new legislation (Nov 2004) will mean that your landlord/agent is going to have to be much more proactive about preventing tenants from deciding to sublet a spare room. Where most turned a blind eye before when couples sublet the spare bedroom to help with costs, landlords are likely to keep a beady eye on this situation *now*.

Increasing the number of tenants to three non-related individuals can now bring quite small units under a fairly costly new licensing process that most landlords/agents will, quite understandably, want to avoid. Expect no subletting clauses in smaller units to be much tighter in the near future so don't take on a unit that will need a hidden lodger to make the sums add up.

# Renting in groups

Some very specific and important advice is needed for people who rent together in a group. Other information is required for tenants who, as individuals, rent a room, or a part of a house, which they share with others. This is a very complex area. More detailed advice is available in the Lesson 7 and also in the Lesson 14 on houses in multiple occupation.

Read it all, because if you fall into any of these categories (i.e there's several of you living on one lease) some additional safety standards may apply to you. If you are viewing a multi-occupied property, or a property which has been converted into flats or bedsits, you really need to read the extra chapters too. I'm delighted to say that the government has (after a long period of consultation) introduced new legislation in the Housing Act 2004, which now clarifies the law that governs safety in multi-occupied accommodation. Things are looking up.

## *Sorting out the issues*

So, use your common sense. Try to assess the arrangements on offer and how they will work in practice. Some landlords and agents are trying to create multi-occupy properties in ways which can be difficult to live with. Four people, no matter how well they get on, living in a three bedroom house, with one of them occupying the only living room, can cause problems because of lack of social space. Similarly three friends sharing the rent equally, while one has the master bedroom and the other two have smaller ones, can cause real friction.

Sort out these issues *before* you sign any leases. There may be no alternative, but you ought to be aware in advance that it can be problematic. You are signing a legally binding contract, usually with a six-month fixed term. This gives you your share of legal liabilities. You will not be able to walk away from it in three months if the mood takes you or you fall out with your pals. In just the same way that your landlord cannot ask you to leave just because they feel like a change, you will also suffer significant financial penalties if you choose to terminate early.

You also need to consider when sharing property, again before conflict arises, how shared bills will be met, as the following anecdote illustrates.

> **WARNING ANECDOTE**
>
> Four men sharing a four bedroom house ought not to sound problematic. However, in order to generate more rent, the landlord divided the accommodation oddly. Two tenants each had a bedroom plus a sitting room with a gas fire, and two had only a bedroom. All shared the only kitchen and bathroom. Obviously, the two double room lets were charged more rent. However, all were asked to share the bills equally. Clearly, the tenants with the cheaper accommodation were contributing more than their fair share, as they were paying towards their fellow tenants' sitting rooms' running costs with roaring fake gas fires. It caused massive friction, yet each had signed contracts accepting this. Whenever a single room occupant vacated early, usually due to arguments, a new tenant accepted the same terms. Over the three years this arrangement ran, every time a tenant became frustrated by the unfairness of the arrangement and vacated early, the landlord refused to refund the deposit, and simply re-let.

### The rooming house arrangement

Enquire before you accept any shared accommodation, especially in a multi-occupied house with fellow tenants who are unknown to you, how the bills are organised. Many well-run 'rooming houses', recognising the problems, include all energy bills in the rent. If you are obliged to share bills, be very wary. If you are to be individually charged, the best arrangement is for individual meters. There are legal limits on the profits landlords can make on the resale of fuel to tenants. You can find about these from the Citizens' Advice Bureaux.

Where energy or water is included in the rent, your landlord must pay these bills. Sometimes tenants can find that they are threatened with disconnection because their landlord has not paid the account. In this instance, *immediately* contact your local council's private tenants officer or the Citizens' Advice Bureaux for advice. They have some powers to help.

# Lesson 3

# Deposits

Ah, the *deposits*! For almost two decades tenants have struggled with the current system as strangers dipped their sticky fingers into this lucrative honeypot. Conservative estimates quote figures of tens of millions each year stolen or misappropriated by agents and landlords alike. So, heaven be praised, the government has finally acted. A Tenancy Deposit Scheme came into in operation on 6 April 2007 and woe betide the landlords who don't obey this new rule.

However, and it's a big *however,* introducing all the systems to get a scheme as big as this off the ground has been an enormous task and, in truth, the system may still be subject to delays and hiccups. However, credit where it's due. The old system was a mess. A better system is long overdue and now things should begin improving for tenants and landlords.

> However, for landlords and tenants alike, the only way to make either old or new deposit systems actually work is to have some accurate *record* of conditions on acceptance. Make sure that you have a new inventory – one that you've checked and agreed as accurate. Many landlords now take digital photos of units – and what's good for the goose … Get a record of events on day one and you'll have less problems proving your case at the end of your tenancy.

Because I can only show you the broad principles in a guide that covers so much ground, I'm going to begin this lesson with a few website addresses. Familiarise yourself with them. Keep an eye on progress as free booklets are beginning to be released. www.communities.gov.uk/tenancy.deposits. Run through the links under Housing. Another particularly good site is a landlord site – it's the RLA (Residential Landlords Association) and this has a great Q&A session that anyone can understand at www.rla.org.uk. Alternatively your Citizens' Advice Bureau will (hopefully) soon have details, or if you get stuck ring your local council, explain what you need and they'll find someone in the private rental sector department to help you.

Eventually, I have every confidence that the government will soon have one of their excellent booklets. Until then, it's web web web.

Meanwhile I'll do the best I can to explain:

- The old system that will still affect many of you with existing deposits already held by landlords/agents.

- Brief principles of the new scheme for all deposits on assured shorthold tenancies from 6 April 2007, along with other reputable sources where more than my snapshot can be checked through.

- Pitfalls that might cause problems for tenants with the new system.

## Who deposits belong to

Whenever you decide to rent a property, now or under any new scheme, you will be required to pay a deposit against damage and unpaid bills during and after your tenancy. This deposit belongs to tenants. It doesn't now, nor did it ever, belong to landlords/agents. Unfortunately, many people didn't seem to appreciate that legal nicety. Hence the need for new legal protections for tenants.

> Deposit deductions can only be reasonable charges
> for *unreasonable* conduct.

If you are asked to pay a deposit of more than two months' rent, you really need to take some specialist advice. You may be able to claim that you have paid a 'premium', which confers some additional legal rights. It's most unlikely to happen if you use an experienced landlord or agent so be warned, life is easier if tenants do business with a landlord who knows the current rules.

### The carrot and stick principle

All landlords/agents need a deposit in order to safeguard the contents and condition of the property they are letting out. There *are* tenants who abuse property. Tenants who leave behind a trail of bad debts, which can leave new tenants facing nightmares with their own credit or fending off bailiffs. Tenants who really expect someone else to scrape a year's fat from the cooker and scrub behind the loo for free when they leave. You name it, all landlords have seen it. A deposit is our only protection against this. What seems to have got lost somewhere is the **carrot** concept, the idea that, given a nice clean flat to start with and a thorough inventory agreed by both parties, tenants do clear up *in order* to get their much needed deposit back.

Of course, the vast majority of tenants do *not* damage property. On the contrary, most do their level best to ensure that property is returned in good order simply because they really *need* the deposit refund. Most obtain a full refund. Many obtain a part refund (though many experience vastly inflated 'charges'). What the legislators are seeking to prevent are inflated costs and to protect the ten per cent of tenants who get nothing back at all. Because ten per cent nationally is an *awful* lot of cash going walkies.

Under the existing system, getting money back from people doing their level best to stop you is where the fun and games so often start.

## How deposits work

By the day you move in at the latest, and under both old and new systems, the landlord's full deposit will be required (though this may be taken by the agent).

If you are asked for **key money**, this is a separate, additional charge. Avoid it. It's a throwback to the days when the deposits held were only token sums. You need a landlord who's up to date with all these new rules, not one still running things in the 1950s.

Check how the deposit needs to be provided. Some landlords require cash (but only usually for relatively cheaper units). Some agents and landlords prefer cheques, banker's drafts or building society cheques. Ask what is required for your property, plus when and how it needs to be paid. It must always be paid in time for funds *to clear* before you are allowed to sign leases. However a deposit is requested you must always insist on having a separate receipt for your deposit, and *keep it safe*.

> This sum of money is held by your landlord/agent as security. Many of the disputes which arise do so simply because people have either failed to understand what was expected of them, or chosen to ignore what was required of them. This convenient amnesia applies to both landlords *and* tenants.

### Reasonable deductions

Deductions can obviously be expected to be made if you make a cigarette burn in the carpet. Deductions cannot be made if a hole wears in the carpet, as this is 'wear and tear'. Routine redecoration cannot be charged for. However if you damage the decorations in any way, you will be charged for part or full redecoration. If you decide to repaint the walls, the landlord/agency can, and probably will, charge you for the cost of returning the property to the owner's preferred colour. Electric kettles, which wear out or break during normal use cannot be charged for. Ones that you have boiled dry and made the element melt can and will be. Ditto drains blocked by fat or toilets jammed with . . . well whatever.

If you leave the place dirty or with damage, cleaning, repair and replacements are not cheap when done by contractors – landlords aren't your devoted parents. We don't work for love.

However . . .

> **WARNING ANECDOTE**
>
> A leading London firm of letting agents (and member of the most widely known voluntary lettings associations) made the national press recently for charging outgoing tenants cleaning rates of £125.00 per hour! This clear abuse should be stopped in its tracks by the new Tenancy Deposit Scheme but that's of little comfort to tenants with existing deposits held by agents with such cavalier attitudes to other people's hard earned money.

Tenants with genuine abuse on their hands have, until the establishment of the new scheme, only had access to the Small Claims Court, thus tying the disputed funds up for months on end. Winning eventually is small consolation when a decent tenant needs the old deposit to fund their next rental. And of little interest I suspect to an industry grown fat on high charges for everything they could possibly excuse as chargeable.

Nevertheless, if you believe that, under the old system, you have been either overcharged or unfairly treated by any landlord or their agent, use the Small Claims Court system. It's cheap, simple and highly effective. Look up Courts in your *Yellow Pages*, ring and ask for forms for a claim. Court staff can't give you legal advice, but they are very helpful at getting you off on the right track. Alternatively, everything can be done online.

---

### WARNING ANECDOTE

Tenants really do have to come to terms with reading and understanding their leases thoroughly. If for example you move into a flat which is badly in need of redecoration, do take care that your landlord hasn't inserted a 'tenants' responsibility for decorating' clause buried somewhere in your lease. If the garden looks like a wilderness, avoid an insertion in the lease to 'maintain' it. You're actually being obligated to improve your landlord's property, while paying them for the privilege and tenants can rarely afford to challenge unscrupulous landlords.

---

## Read that lease

And preferably before you sign it! If you don't understand something, ask for an explanation. Because whatever you've agreed to will be in your lease and you'll be held to it.

*Every single time you decide to hang a picture with a hammer and nail*, think carefully about your precious deposit. In some instances you can lose huge sums of money, especially in expensive properties where well-plastered walls don't look their best with inches of shattered plaster. Fitting a unit or shelves to the wall, or having a cable TV system installed, may seem like excellent ideas...until you come to remove them when you leave. You will be charged for all damages you cause installing permanent fixtures. In some cases these fitted items can actually become the property of your landlord. Always remember, landlords/agents exist to make a profit. The arrangement you have entered is purely commercial, and your deposit can and *will* be utilised to pay the genuine cost of any repairs necessary *as a result of your conduct.*

> Remember, your contact is effectively temporary. That should inform you better than anything else about how you must *live* as an assured shorthold tenant.

**WARNING ANECDOTE**

A young tenant wanted to put up a mirror in the bedroom of a lovely student house. Carefully, with a craft knife, he removed four small triangles of the wallpaper, drilled and plugged the wall, and hung his mirror. On leaving, he removed the mirror, opened a tobacco tin in which 18 months previously he had carefully stored the four small triangles, removed the plugs, filled the holes, glued the triangles back in place, and left the flat. He received a full deposit return.

Interestingly, *The Telegraph* reviewer for a previous edition of this guide mocked this anecdote merrily as inconceivable. However all my anecdotes are true. It wasn't 'inconceivable' at all – this tenant was actually my own son who'd been involved in letting since his teens and who knew all about tenancy deposits, while renting accommodation from Edinburgh University.

## Doing 'little jobs around the place'

So try to remember that story whenever you decide to do 'a little job' in any rented property. These contracts are tight, and you need to be *very* careful. If you think that a bathroom without a mirror will be a problem (and who wouldn't?) ask the landlord/agent to put one up before you move in or find a more realistically equipped unit. If agents/landlords give permission for alterations, ask for it in writing. (Sorting details like this via email is a brilliant way for tenants to create a paper trail without raising hackles.)

# The system for deposits taken before 6 April 2007

Deposits and deductions from them are a hugely contentious area – meaning that I am trying to advise you across a huge variety of practice: from the small landlord who respects their tenants' realities, to the big agents, responsible to nothing but a high level of profitability, no matter how they achieve their targets. (What I say in this section will largely remain the case under any deposit system. Only the way your deposit is held and how disputes are resolved are changing.)

## Under the pre-April 2007 system

No landlord or agent has any right whatsoever to deduct any of your deposit without good cause. Familiarise yourself with both this Lesson and Lesson 4 on inventories. Then you should be better protected from some of their worst practices until the new Tenancy Deposit Scheme is in place.

## When will I get my deposit back?

There is often a time lag between leaving and receiving any deposit return. A short delay of several days is quite reasonable. Landlords and agents *have* to check that all outstanding bills and accounts associated with your tenancy have been settled before they organise refunds. Of course, if you leave the property without having given proper notice, or before the end of the fixed term, your deposit will almost always be utilised to cover rent owed (at least until your landlord has found a satisfactory replacement tenant).

Some landlords do manage to get back deposits very promptly, but never expect a landlord to hand over your deposit before they've had a chance to check that you've paid all your bills, let alone as you move out. Many will do their best to get money back quickly, but no landlord is a hole in the wall.

## Protect your deposit

Tenants must learn how best to protect their deposit rather than throwing it away then complaining vociferously afterwards. Damage will always be charged for – and the cost of workmen can make your eyes bleed – you have been warned!

Coffee spilled on beds and carpets is *not* routine wear and tear, but *damage*. Expect to be charged. Cigarette burns, dirty beds, brown toilets – someone has to clean them up before a new tenant can move in. Therefore tenants who took a nice clean building have to don rubber gloves and get scrubbing before they move out. Just running a Hoover over the middle of the carpets is not enough. Toilets, inside cookers and fridges, bathroom floors, under beds and yes, windows, all need to be washed before you go. Don't forget to replace light bulbs.

And again, another word of warning, put everything back where you found it. I know plenty of landlords who'll throw a couple of hours freebie at a unit just to get it straight back on the market and save hassle, but agents have multiple subsidiary companies just aching for you to leave a mess, and cause some redecorating and they charge top whack for everything.

### Interest on your deposit under the old system

A basic legal principle applies to tenancy deposits. Many tenants do not realise that they are entitled to interest on their deposits. Your entitlement is at wholesale bank deposit rate, which you can find out through your own branch, or from your citizens' advisory services. Do make a claim for this money at the end of your tenancy. Just imagine how much interest the tenants' deposits in a nationally based estate or lettings agents are generating every year if no one even asks for it back.

Unfortunate changes are underway to fund the new system.

## The new Tenancy Deposit Scheme from 6 April 2007

Just to confuse matters there are *two* new types of tenancy deposit protection 'schemes', each of which operates in slightly different ways. Your landlord/agent (*not you*) decides where to safeguard your deposit under whichever scheme they prefer. All that's legally required is that they use *a* scheme. These new rules apply *to every single deposit* taken on an assured shorthold lease (in other words the overwhelming majority of tenancies) after 6 April 2007. Since that date all assured shorthold deposits need, by law, to be safeguarded under one type or another of tenancy deposit schemes.

It's the landlord's/agent's job to find out about schemes and how to use them, not the tenant's. Strict penalties exist in tenants' favour against landlords/agents who don't protect your deposit. All tenants are legally entitled to official documentation of where their deposit is 'safeguarded' within 14 days of handing over a tenancy deposit. So, ask for the paperwork. It's yours by law. However, where there's clarity on some things, others are much less clear as you'll see.

> Please do check out the websites I've given throughout this Lesson, they'll add to your understanding of what are some of the biggest changes ever seen in the UK letting market. The information in this guide can only give you enough to know what to look out for as the new systems gear up for business.

*Note*

The government is *not* holding deposits – this powerful position is to be given to private companies who will – sigh – need to make a profit on deposit management.

## Option 1 the insurance based scheme

Based on nothing more than a hunch – I suspect that this scheme will prove the more popular with independent landlords. My reasoning? It feels much more familiar than option 2 (explained in a minute).

Under this scheme landlords will choose a supplier of 'guarantees' i.e. a company that insures their tenants' deposits and the landlord/agent will then pay some form of joining fee. When a tenant hands over a deposit under this system, landlords will continue to hold onto it. They will however have to also do the following things.

■ Landlords/agents will be legally obliged to register this specific deposit and (presumably) pay an additional charge to their insurer to specifically insure the sum of your deposit.

■ This must be done within 14 days of accepting any deposit (on an assured shorthold tenancy) (14 days after receipt of deposit – not 14 days into the tenancy).

■ Having registered the deposit as held, the landlord's/agent's chosen insurer will then issue paperwork to the tenant via the landlord. This document must state exactly who is safeguarding your deposit where they can be reached, etc and documentation *must reach you* within those 14 days.

If everything proceeds well, the insurers will have little to do. Landlords and tenants will have to discuss deposit refunds together. A novel idea for many!

■ If a full refund is due the landlord is obliged to refund your money within ten days, but can do so much earlier as they have access to it.

■ If any deductions are required, these must be *agreed* with the tenant before a penny of your deposit is touched.

■ If *mutual agreement* is reached about how much can fairly be deducted to cover agreed costs, the landlord is again obliged to refund the deposit balance within ten days.

So, theoretically, under this scheme so long as landlords and tenants behave themselves they should be able to sort all these matters out amicably. That way, a legal maximum of ten days should occur between leaving any unit and getting back the money you are genuinely owed.

### *Disputes*

*Only* if disputes arise will the safeguarding insurance company need to become significantly involved. So, if landlord and tenant do *not* agree how much deposit deduction can fairly be made, they must engage in a legal process.

■ At the stage of *any dispute* the landlord/agent will be legally obliged to inform their insurance service immediately.

■ *And landlords must hand over the whole of the disputed amount* to their insuring company immediately. Make sure that your landlord knows that you are aware of this – and of their obligations.

■ Any undisputed balance must be handed back to the tenant within ten days.

So, say your landlord holds a £600 deposit and you are at loggerheads over a proposed £200 deposit deduction, then the landlord must immediately hand over the disputed £200 to their insurance scheme *and* return the undisputed £400 to you direct within ten days.

■ With disputed money safely back in the hands of the company safeguarding your deposit a dispute resolution service will kick in. Schemes, not the landlord, will decide who owes what to whom and it will disperse money accordingly. Of course, first both landlord and tenant must jointly agree to *use* the dispute resolution service – unless they do, arguing parties will be back to the small claims courts – and the scheme will hold onto the money, then only disperse it according to a court's ruling. Courts, I suspect, will not be delighted to see claimants who've refused to use a perfectly fair arbitration system.

The insurance aspect of these schemes means that defaulting landlords will no longer be able to abscond with tenants' cash. The insurer will pay out what is owed to tenants direct and it will be responsible for chasing up its debtor landlords/agents – not tenants via the Small Claims Courts. Applause!

### Advantages of the new system

Now if all this seems complicated – that's because it is a bit. But it's a whole lot better protection than tenants have ever had before and that can only be good news all round. We'll all soon get used to these changes and won't be able to believe we ever relied on the existing roughshod system.

> Tenants will be able to chase up their own deposits because they'll know where they are safeguarded without having to face endless argy bargy with a landlord who may or may not have a fair case.

These systems will also involve tenants in a new way. Adult negotiation between parties is to be encouraged to avoid disputes. So too is the new realisation for tenants that they can't leave a totally decimated dump in their wake then threaten the landlord with court if he doesn't pay up on the spot, then clean up for free.

## Option 2 the custodial scheme

This is a single national scheme: the Deposit Protection Service. Contact www.depositprotection.com. Again despite the service style name, this is another purely commercial organisation, part of Computershare Investor Services Plc. Unfortunately, this service is not being paid for by fees from landlords/agents, but – believe it or not – from the interest generated by *tenants'* deposits. So I guess that any interest returns to tenants will take a nosedive. Ho hum.

Under this system, landlords/agents will simply put the entire deposit into the single national custodial scheme immediately (or as before within 14 days of receipt). And again, tenants have a legal right to specific documentation telling them exactly where their precious deposit is being safeguarded. End of tenancy situations will be very similar to the ones explained earlier – except where landlords/agents use this scheme, do not expect instant refunds as a whole system needs to be gone through before tenants' money is refunded.

Again, I expect the ten-day norm to bed down and that's a long time for many tenants. The process with disputed deposits will be similar and offer a dispute resolution service as an option instead of court. And again, both parties must at least be able to agree to use arbitration.

To help you understand this system, try contacting your Citizens' Advice Bureau, the local authority's private lettings officer or www.tds.gb.com who have very helpful telephone staff, on 0845 226 7837.

### Obvious pitfalls

I'm not alone in making sure that good tenants who've cleared up get a full deposit refund a jolly sight quicker than ten days. Many tenants need their old deposit to fund their new one – that's why they did such a good clear up. Now, there's nothing in the insurance based system to prevent this from happening with landlords who held onto deposits, but I am concerned that prompt deposit refunds will become even rarer and ten days become the norm.

My second concern is more serious. I've come across some pretty unsavoury characters who love lettings because it generates a low profile, high *control*, cash only business. Tenants may find themselves pushed by some landlords into accepting a higher deposit deduction than is fair by the threat of tying funds up for some time in a system. When tenants are as cash strapped as they often are, this type of threat – especially where large deposit deductions are being demanded – may well intimidate tenants into accepting a lower refund on the spot. We shall see. But I wish I'd seen a way round this discussed on any of the official websites, who still seem in complete denial about the some of the characters who've been attracted to being landlords over the decades.

My third concern is how I wish that our legislators lived in the real world, where everyone wasn't some 'nice, reasonable guy' (above) who'd happily comply with a new law – indeed with *any* lettings law. The *very* tenants who suffer lousy landlords (usually those at the bottom of the cash pile) are the worst placed people of all to tackle a strapping landlord who fails to safeguard their deposit – especially on six months' security of tenure! How in the world a tenant enforces this with some landlords is beyond my powers of imagination. Theoretically, you can challenge them.

> My best advice therefore is that you *ask* any landlord/agent which scheme they'll be safeguarding your deposit under *before* you hand any money over in the first place! If they don't have an answer – try and find yourself another unit where the management is more law abiding.

## Reasonable behaviour for both parties

Reading this lesson has already shown what will *always* be reasonable conduct on both sides of these contracts.

- Look for a unit that someone cares for, then respect that in how you live there.

- Make sure that you know enough about the new 2007 mandatory scheme to protect your deposit.

- Don't do home improvement!

- Cleaning up after you isn't a miraculous quid pro quo. You'll get a hefty bill – calling in a team of cleaners to get a place shipshape for reletting costs real money.

It costs four hours labour *minimum* to clean out a disgusting cooker. Hours to redecorate and get carpets professionally cleaned if you spilled coffee all over them or never took off your shoes when they were dirty.

Very often, tenants see the true costs of cleaning up, redecorating or replacing a bed as theft, when the reality is that household work, repairs and decorating cost huge sums of money – the kind of money that tenants simply hadn't appreciated. However, in truth, this isn't actually a finance issue. Some of my most glowing references have been written for people who had relatively modest weekly budgets, but cared about their environment, respected other people's property and never had any difficulty in working out that clean meant really, really clean.

### One final tip

If you live as promised and get a full deposit refund, ask your old landlord/agent for a personal reference. The *only* piece of paper that I and most independent landlords take seriously is a glowing reference from someone else who's rented out to you before – they're worth more than gold!

# Lesson 4

# Inventories

The preceding chapter covered the payment of your deposit. In this section we will be dealing with the contents and conditions, which your deposit is designed to protect because inventories and deposits are intimately tied together.

Almost certainly you will be asked to agree and to sign an inventory, which will usually form the basis upon which your deposit return will, amongst other things, be based. Your inventory is absolutely essential, and will, if managed properly, safeguard your own, as well as your landlord's, interests. Read it, check it and only sign what you agree is accurate.

Very occasionally you will be offered a property without a written inventory, and where this does happen it can be a very mixed blessing indeed. Without an inventory, *neither* party can actually prove what the original contents were, nor their original condition. While at first glance you may feel happy about accepting a property without any inventory, remember that you are far more likely than the landlord to have to use the courts in the event of a dispute, and you will have no proof of the original condition.

So, you might sensibly be wondering why your landlord doesn't want to provide one of the most important documents of all. And it's a foolish landlord indeed who skips this part of the process. Tenants without inventories are perfectly placed to deny any or all damage and, without an accurate signed document the landlord doesn't have many legal legs to balance his argument on.

## Types of inventory

Let us however assume that an inventory has been produced, and consider how and by whom it has been drawn up.

### Independent inventories

Many expensive properties, and indeed some fairly average ones, are offered with the benefit of an independent inventory, usually compiled by a specialist company. This arrangement has the advantage of being much more impartial than other types. When you vacate, the same company will complete a leaving check and assess if any damages or negligence (or home improvement!) have arisen. They will often also calculate the costs required to cover problems (often providing estimates), and advise the landlord or agency in writing of their findings. You should also be able to obtain a copy of both reports.

This is a highly satisfactory arrangement, and while it can seem expensive (the costs are often shared between landlord and tenant), it has the undoubted advantage of independence.

> Any tenant renting property with a relatively high rent is strongly urged to also consider the advantages of this type of service.

Tenants in high-rent areas, even where they have already been charged by their agent or landlord for alternative 'in-house' services, should very seriously consider the advantages of paying for their own independent assessment at lease beginning and end. In central London for example, some rents are thousands of pounds per month, and this is a sensible safeguard for what will be a significant deposit. If you decide to cover your back with an independent inventory, arrange this for before you unpack. Provide the landlord/agent with a copy of the document – this in itself will usually be sufficient to discourage many end of lease shenanigans.

### In-house inventories

More usual are agencies whose own staff draw up the inventory, and conduct the final inspection. Remember that for agents and private landlords alike, there's no quality control on the production of any legally binding inventory – nor any genuine guidelines to follow. It's an ad hoc service – sometimes, but not always, done very con-scientiously.

An obvious note of caution here is that many agencies run a number of smaller companies/operations within the overall service offered to landlords, e.g. cleaning companies, or decorating or gardening services. A sceptic might just consider the possible advantages in finding problems with the condition of the property once you have vacated. This is a highly lucrative sideline for many operators, and there is no independent scrutiny of agencies, nor are there any qualifications required before you can set one up.

> If you have left the property as you accepted it, you should expect your money back. Challenge any unreasonably high or unfair charges on existing deposits.

Further advice on this is given in Lesson 10. All these issues should begin to be much fairer with the introduction of the new Tenancy Deposit Scheme discussed in the earlier Lesson on deposits.

### *Privately landlord inventories*

Compiled by private landlords, these inventories (as above) can be either highly competent documents, or brief, handwritten scrawls. The same warning about objectivity applied to in-house inventories should also be applied here. They may be free, or chargeable. Ask.

Sensible service providers need accurate records and so do tenants I always now take digital photos of properties on moving in day and ask tenants to sign them as accurate. Tenants too could do exactly the same thing and get them developed with a dateline. Get yourself some evidence of the original condition of rented property – under both existing and new systems of deposit systems, evidence can save you money.

Here's an excerpt of a very simple inventory to give you some idea of what to expect. Many are much more detailed – some much less so.

**Kitchen**
All fitted units and cupboards clean
Cooker – clean on acceptance
Refrigerator – cleaned and defrosted on acceptance
Microwave – clean

1 pair small chequered curtains plus curtain pole and rings (clean)

1 small net curtain (please wash and re-hang on vacation)

Vinyl floor covering (in good condition)

Service automatic washing machine/dryer (service contract details in top drawer)

C/H boiler (landlord's gas safety certificate (tenant copy) plus service contract details in top drawer)

Fitted chrome towel rail

Light fittings (3 halogen bulbs fitted and working)

1 smoke detector (batteries working)

1 carbon monoxide detector (batteries working)

1 domestic sized fire extinguisher and fire blanket

Many of us separate the contents and the building, therefore a schedule of building condition may be part of your inventory package and may look something like this.

**Lounge**

Walls – plain cream, plastered and emulsioned finish. Unmarked except for small areas of damage behind sofa head. Three picture hooks provided. Please fix *nothing* extra to the walls (including pins and bluetac), as they damage the decorative finish.

Stripped floorboards in good condition with the exception of a small area of wear damage between bay window and hallway

1 casement window – in working order with working catches and window locks (key on LHS window sill of bay).

Paintwork – white gloss, several small chips to doorframe otherwise in good condition throughout.

Ceiling – white emulsion, unmarked

## What to check

However formal or informal, these inventories are meant to represent the contents of the property, and the condition of its contents on moving in day. In some instances they also state the decorative condition of the premises you are about to rent (schedule of condition). You need to check any documents you are asked to sign extremely carefully. Too often, embarrassed tenants simply smile at the landlord and say they're sure it's OK. This has happened to me many times. I always insist that tenants both read and check the inventory because it is our *mutual* protection.

Draw any deficiencies (if anything's been missed by accident) to the attention of the landlord/ agent. If you are asked to sign an inventory in an agency office having *previously* visited the property, ask to revisit before signing a thing – you must check the property conditions against the inventory and don't take no for an answer.

Signing accurate inventories is a vitally important part of your deposit return process that can't be skipped if at all possible. If you find for example that the inventory simply says 'sofa' but you can see a couple of cigarette burns or it looks slightly soiled, ask politely for this to be noted on the inventory. If you meet with a refusal to change the inventory, start asking yourself why.

This process can actually take a little time. Some landlords and agents can look rather pained if you want to be thorough. Ignore the clearing of throats and glancing at watches that can accompany this process, and don't sign anything just to get hold of the property. Obvious deficiencies can truly come back to haunt you in this business.

> Having read and agreed the contents of your inventory, you will be expected to sign it as a true reflection of the property at the time you took possession of it. Once you've done this, you're stuck with that statement – there's no going back. Ask for your own copy and keep it safe. As emphasised before, these are important, legally binding documents, which need careful storage.

## *Inventory safeguards*

Property is expensive – and so are its contents. Responsible landlords/ agents ensure that their paperwork is accurate. But the unwary fall victim to scams too numerous to mention. Here's a tale from a leading financial journalist passed over to me only last month.

> **WARNING ANECDOTE**
>
> Tenants had contacted a leading newspaper concerned about various aspects of their tenancy, not least charges being levied when a new tenant moved in. However, what interested me most was the inventory process suggested by the agent. A new tenant would move in, no mid-term inspection would be undertaken and the old inventory condition would be 'assumed'. Meaning that the outgoing tenant could, in fact, be walking away from considerable damage uncharged as a simple deposit switch was planned. However, what stunned these tenants more was their sudden realisation that they'd never seen an inventory – much less signed one. Apparently the agent was still relying on an inventory taken six years earlier and signed by a completely unknown group of strangers.

Inventories matter. Properties that don't automatically generate new, accurate inventories will be problematic simply because you'll be dealing with someone who is either not sure what they're doing, or someone deliberately trying to undermine your deposit rights. Rent property that comes with an accurate paper-trail. If you really can't – then at the end of this Lesson I tell you how to draw up a document of your own that could well help to protect your interests.

## Safeguarding your deposit

This all sounds so easy, doesn't it? Ask to visit the property, take the inventory, have all the time you want to examine it, ask for anything that concerns you to be included on it before you sign, and bingo, you're all set!

The reality can sometimes be a little different, as every relatively experienced tenant reading this will know. This particularly applies at the lower end of the price range. You may be renting a property with stains too numerous to mention on the furniture. You may be struggling to find something which you can afford, and the agent is telling you that he has eight other people interested! You may very well, on this type of property, *never even see a* written inventory.

### Enter the reality zone for many tenants

Because property in certain price ranges (usually the cheapest) is in very high demand the last thing you can afford to seem is picky. The truth is that the last thing some landlords and agents *want* is a tenant trying to look after their own interests. You may not get the property at all if you start asking for paperwork – or even if you sound well informed. The truth can often be that your options are limited by what you can afford to pay. Not everyone's a high flyer with a six-figure salary. The majority of rentals are mid-range and only affordable when shared and a sizeable chunk of our industry operates way down the pay-scales.

Sometimes tenants find that they have little alternative but to take a property that they know is less than ideal. In these circumstances, a slightly different approach may help and it certainly can't hurt.

> If you are going to accept the property irrespective of the condition, you still need quietly to protect your interests. Even a modest house, or flat in most cities, will be holding a deposit of hundreds of pounds, and you need to be able to get it back.

It is too often forgotten that for some of us, at certain times in our lives, the loss of even a hundred pounds can cause a great deal of hardship. It should also be remembered that most tenants have to plan and save for, or even borrow, the deposits on their rented homes. The unfair loss of even a proportion of it can trap people in a cycle of poor quality housing, because their deposit return is vital to fund the new deposit on a slightly better option.

This can be oppressive, and tenants in these circumstances need to act thoroughly to protect their own interests. You may, for example, have no alternative but to sign an inventory, which simply gives a list of items, with no indication of their condition. It may state 'all items in good clean condition', when they are not.

### Ways to help yourself

Here are a few practical tips which can genuinely help. Take someone with you, preferably *not* a relative or a close friend, who can give independent evidence should you need it about how things really were when you moved in. Take a photocopy of the inventory you have signed and, on the first day of your tenancy, note every problem on your own copy of the inventory and *post the photocopy*, (never part with original documents) via registered post to your landlord or agent. A neighbour who isn't the landlord's tenant and who isn't concerned may be prepared to take a look around and support your word on how things were when you moved in.

## Create a valid paper trail to protect your deposit

The following is a procedure that is always worth following if you do not have the security of an *independent* inventory service − or indeed have taken on a property that didn't come with a fresh, accurate inventory. This applies to property right across the price range. Don't make the common mistake of assuming that top notch rent equals top notch conduct from management − or assume the new TDS will be able to help without evidence.

- On the day that you take possession, as your first task go through the whole property thoroughly, either with your inventory, which you have signed, or making your own paper record (something similar to the suggestions earlier in the lesson).

- Make a careful note of everything in the property, and make a particular note of everything which is already damaged, marked or broken.

- If mould is evident, make a note of its position and extent. It is horribly common in cheap-end rented property. Mould on the walls (black circular dots that rub away with a fingertip, leaving a residual stain) can ruin your belongings as it is impossible to wash out. It can also play havoc with your health!

- Make a detailed list of everything which concerns you, e.g. cooker rings that are loose or do not work, stains on beds, coffee-ring stains on tables, loose sockets, etc.

- Detail the state of the decorations, including whether or not they are in good condition.

- Sign and date the inventory/schedule and if at all possible, get a witness signature.

- Beg borrow or . . . well whatever . . . get hold of a digital camera and take photos of any damaged items, putting that day's newspaper headline and date clearly and visibly in the picture.

- Have your photographs processed immediately, a same-day service is best and may even show a dateline.

- Place your detailed list plus your photographs in an envelope within 24 hours, and *mail them registered post to yourself at your new address*.

- When the envelope is delivered put it somewhere very safe, but on no account open it. I repeat, don't break the seal.

It's been my experience that deposit deductions are a bit like buses, they come along in groups. If a landlord/agent thinks you won't kick up too much fuss they can start piling on the charges. Don't accept this. If you damaged something (and accidents do happen) admit it – but don't then feel pressurised to accept everything but the kitchen sink being thrown at you. I hate to say it, but these situations are far too common industry-wide. Twenty years ago, being a private landlord was a practical way for people to earn their own income. These days it's a wish list for the fast living, easy buck brigade. Don't let a well cut suit or crystal vowels intimidate you. Your rent pays everyone's wages – remember?

### Using your evidence

If there is any dispute when you come to leave the property about exactly what condition various things were in when you took possession, simply tell the landlord or agent that you took the precaution of obtaining proof. Do not at any stage either give them the envelope or break the seal, but *explain* what steps you took to protect your deposit. This will be valuable evidence if you need to go to court or any deposit resolution service over any dispute, and landlords and agents will recognise this very quickly!

> With this unopened document in place, you've done the best you can to record and date the true conditions when you moved in. This should prove invaluable if the first time that envelope seal is broken is by any arbitrator or court and you have postage proof with dates.

What's more, the total cost is about £5, which isn't much for the protection – let alone your peace of mind – is it?

### Why bother – isn't this new deposit system going to sort out these problems?

Even when the new deposit system is up and running, arbitrators or courts will always be looking for documentary proof. It is amazing to me that tenants don't take more steps to protect themselves. I can't imagine any other circumstances where intelligent people would hand over hundreds/thousands of pounds to someone they have only known for a matter of minutes, trusting the integrity of a virtual stranger on the basis of a handwritten receipt and an in-house inventory.

> Tenants should try to be *proactive.*

By reading this and spending a few minutes once a year when you move, you could ensure that you are not always on the back foot where deposit refunds are concerned. The lettings business isn't always a nice place filled with reasonable people. It's a cold commercial concern where people are out to make a profit – from you!

Always remember that those landlords/agents engaging in sharp practice are relying on your lack of knowledge, or forward planning. They cannot exploit well-prepared tenants. Unfair deposit deductions tend to rely on your ignorance or timidity. Nor will any new system work well if *neither* party has bothered to do anything to show accurately how things were when you first accepted the property. Frankly, you have two choices. Let someone walk away with your hard earned money or *do* something to protect your own interests. I know what I'd do eight days a week!

# Lesson 5

# How to manage landlord/agency relationships

One of the trickiest questions of all for tenants is whether or not they want to do business direct with a private landlord, or whether they'd prefer to use an agency. At the very top end of the market, most property is too expensive to be offered as assured shorthold tenancies – these types of units are managed almost exclusively by agents on entirely different contracts.

## Money matters

Where tenants are paying more than £25,000 per year (£481 per week collectively) in rent, they cannot legally be offered an assured shorthold tenancy. However as rents climb and people increasingly club together to make property affordable, the £25,000 maximum limit for assured shorthold leases is creeping even into the top end of student housing. Any property with rent more than that maximum of £25,000 per year whose tenants have been given an assured shorthold lease should take immediate legal advice. Before you start crying, many, *many* solicitors offer a half-hour free service. Besides that, Housing Law groups exist in every large city. However, the over-whelming majority of rentals do not fall into this super priced bracket.

## Options for the majority: the agent or the private landlord

Broadly, if you want to find accommodation on the high street you'll be using agency management through their many branches, just teeming with rentals. If you prefer to use classified advertising to find a home, which can often be cheaper, you're more likely to be dealing with your landlord direct. Again, the direct supply these days is tremendous.

The rental sector these days is huge. A behemoth. Enormous. The range of management styles reflects this. Some independent landlords manage property brilliantly, without any need for agencies or their costs, which many of us believe actively discourage the very budget conscious type of individuals we are actively seeking for tenants. Many other landlords haven't the time to manage what is, for them, a part-time investment and so use agencies. And every single tenant will have a different experience in whatever type of management they plump for.

■ Agencies are expensive. Their upfront costs can be astronomical.

■ On the other hand, some private landlords who don't make all these upfront demands simply cannot get their heads around leaving a tenant in peace; let alone respecting the 'right of quiet enjoyment' which tenants buy with their rent.

Advising people what to choose or what they'll like best is like pretending to be able to predict someone's favourite flavour. Statistically and practically impossible. So I won't bother. Instead, I will say the same thing that I've said so often before. This is a major financial commitment – use your commonsense.

### Meeting the management

You get an opportunity to meet the management every single time you go to view a property. Either you'll be shown around by an agent or by a private landlord. Whoever you meet is likely to be your 'management'. (This can get a bit confused with agencies who often use viewers to show people around – but make sure that you meet the people who matter some time before you decide who to do business with.) Every time you rent a property, you'll be making a vitally important judgment call based on gut instinct and a few obvious pointers, like:

■ Do you feel happy with the person who's responsible for the management?

■ Have they bothered to clean up before you viewed?

■ Do they seem familiar with the processes?

- Are they well prepared?

- Will they be providing an inventory?

- Can they answer your questions about local authority charges and other costs or don't they have a clue?

- Since April 2007 an excellent new question if you're seriously considering taking the unit is 'which service will be used to hold the deposit'?

- Are they confidently showing you around and explaining how things work, what documents are required, etc?

- Or do they stand, uninterested, by the door?

Landlords who care are usually quite keen to show their unit's advantages off – they've got something for sale and are looking to close a profitable deal.

Go to every viewing with a list of questions that you think are reasonable and try to get a reasonable response (above is a good start, add your own concerns). If answers are not forthcoming, ask yourself seriously if you want that unit enough to take on such a commitment on a scanty response. People who aren't interested before they get your name on a contract won't become considerate landlords/agents after they have your name on a valuable document like a lease.

### Find property that suits your lifestyle

- If it has a huge garden, do you want to spend every weekend mowing the lawn?

- If the high spec kitchen has beautiful wooden worktops, do you want to spend whole days oiling them to keep them watertight?

- How will you stand contractually if you do neither?

- If the property is cheap because the heating is all electric – can you afford the much higher bills?

- If the property has an electric meter (especially pre-pay card types) has the meter been calibrated by the electricity supplier to cover a previous debt by the last tenant? If so, it will need returning to the usual rates before you begin paying.

- If it's an oil-fired heating system, where do you order oil – but not enough to last way beyond your own tenancy?

- If there's insufficient heating, do you really want to use the landlord's lethal paraffin heater?

- If the third bedroom's too small to be any use do you want to pay extra for it?

And on, and on. Before you sign a thing *ask* and then *think*.

### Making that judgement call

We all make instantaneous judgements all the time. It's an instinct thing. Trust it. If the landlord in front of you makes your skin crawl find somewhere else. If the agent can't be bothered, makes you feel that they're doing you a favour by turning out, thinks you're a bore to have important questions – find somewhere else. If there's no adequate reply to who you'd call in emergencies – find somewhere else. You are trying to rent a home, not a car for the weekend. There are things that you need to know are in place because badly managed homes are a nightmare for tenants, who are left holding all the problems with none of the control. Beware the young buccaneering landlord who's only willing to give you a mobile phone number. Get a landline and check it works before you sign leases.

Management of rental property requires organisation, planning and consistency. Someone to call when you lose your keys. Someone to fix the hot water system. You're not allowed to fix things yourself and have already paid for things to work so look for an organised manager – either agency or competent independent – and you shouldn't go too far wrong.

---

**WARNING ANECDOTES**

An old schoolfriend needed somewhere nice to rent for a year in an area she was unfamiliar with. She made two appointments, both through agencies. On neither occasion had the agency bothered to let the existing tenant know that a viewing had been arranged. On one occasion, the agent simply opened up the door without so much as knocking first! Predictably, this tenant was both home and in bed. Tenants (even ones in their final month) have a legal right to be notified that anyone will be coming into what is still their home (24 hours' notice in writing). On both occasions this was flagrantly ignored by two, quite separate agencies. Good management would never walk straight into units without legal notification – let alone without the good manners to knock. Not surprisingly, both units were rejected on management. This experienced lady didn't want keys held by anyone who'd wander in and out of her home without letting her know they were due.

I know a landlady who has earned her income from rentals for more than 45 years. She also chooses to live very nearby her rental properties. An excellent and conscientious landlady who complies with every safety regulation in the book, she has, however, real difficulty with that 'right to quiet enjoyment' aspect. These rentals are 'her property'. On more occasions that I can count, she has lost perfectly good tenants who simply weren't willing to allow her to open their doors and walk in unannounced. Her particular obsession was unopened curtains. If by, say 11 am, the front room curtains were still drawn, she simply walked right in and opened them. One tenant left because she did his dishes while he was at work! Good management lets you live in peace.

Use your commonsense. Look at how existing tenants are treated and you'll get a fairly good flavour of your future as a tenant there.

> TIP If the existing tenant still lives in the unit you're interested in renting, pop back later, without either landlord or agent. Knock on the door and very politely ask them what living there has been like. Works every time!

## Understanding the role of agencies

Agencies are not voluntary organisations who run services for love. They are commercial middlemen who charge whatever they can, to whoever seems likeliest to pay it, because that's commerce. Understanding that will allow you to behave like informed users of the services they offer. So charges will be made for inventory preparation, and for the final inspection when you move out and at every other single opportunity that presents itself in between and after you leave.

All cost top whack – many tenants are charged more than £200 simply for the drawing up and signing of a lease. Understand that from the outset and do your sums accordingly.

> **WARNING ANECDOTE**
>
> A friend recently rented through one of London's poshest agencies. Having agreed a rental the landlord emigrated to China. In an attempt to make a quick buck the agent sent in staff to turn off all services in the three-day gap before tenants moved in. Given the warm summer, the only reason for this was to make a disconnect and reconnect charge to the landlord's account. Unfortunately, their workmen broke a pipe fitting during the reconnect and the whole place flooded, bringing down ceilings and ruining all the parquet flooring. This resulted in an insurance claim between landlord and agent and the costly temporary accommodation of the tenants in one of London's nicer boutique hotels with writs flying overhead like Ken Livingston's displaced pigeons. *Carpe diem* is the best motto for middlemen prospering in *any* service, lettings included. Seize the day sums things up nicely.

## Understanding the role of independent landlords

Again, commerce not community service is the goal of any self-respecting private landlord. Where they differ from agencies is that their costs (not organisational abilities) should be lower because they don't pay middlemen. Few private landlords charge set up fees for the right to take a lease. Most use legal stationers' leases, which cost a couple of pounds, not a couple of hundred. Nor will many consider charging you for three signatures. In a competitive market, few private landlords try to make a profit on references, they use the reference process to safeguard their investment, not for profit.

What you must understand here is the scale of operations you're trying to compare. For most private landlords with, say, a dozen or so properties, a few pounds referencing profit are utterly immaterial – and not worth deterring anyone over. For an agency with many hundreds, even thousands of properties trading each year, these small additional charges everywhere add up to huge revenue generators.

Instead, the private landlord makes his/her money from charging you enough rent to make a profit over and above their own costs. Some will charge inventory fees because they genuinely do take time to compile, agree on and check out. (You need to ask exactly what charges any independent has in mind before agreeing to accept anything.) For expensive units, many will suggest sharing the cost of a completely independent inventory – so no profit there either. Plus, for what it's worth, I've never met one independent landlord who would charge a good tenant wanting to stay beyond six months some 'lease extension fee' for the privilege of having a good customer pay for longer.

## *Rent collections*

Just because agents are happy to assume that your direct debit will actually arrive every month, don't expect all independent landlords to take that view – especially experienced ones. Many landlords live on the income from their units, they're not all some distant investment portfolio but often produce our living. For a multitude of good reasons, many independents prefer the weekly/monthly direct contact with our tenants that rent collection brings. Tenants often have relatively trivial issues they want to raise – like a dripping tap that's keeping them awake every night that might not sound a serious fault in itself, but is causing real frustration. Other times tenants prefer discussing problems about a noisy neighbour with their landlord, sooner than banging on the ceiling.

For any number of reasons, rent collection is still remarkably common, popular and convenient. Many tenants prefer to be able to pay less, more often, too. Plus, not everyone wants to phone some call-centre miles away about a broken lock and hope someone shows to repair it.

> Face to face contact with landlords can be one of the unrecognised benefits of renting through independents.

Of course, you may hate the idea. Like all your other options, these are choices that you make as you work your way through our vast marketplace.

### If it's often cheaper, is there a downside?

Yup. Where disputes arise, you have to discuss these direct with your landlord – there's no buffer. Of course, most tenancies don't have disputes. There's a difference between reporting a fault and chasing someone's tail for a couple of days and all out warfare. Nevertheless, some tenants really are willing to pay a string of supplementary charges for the opportunity to arbitrate through a third party – even one who works for the landlord. Unfortunately, many landlords behave unreasonably just because they can make an agent do their dirty work. Being a letting agent is certainly profitable, but it isn't always comfortable to play pig in the middle.

> As I stressed from the outset, try to find a supplier who you think you can talk to.

Many student landlords are models to us all. They know and like young people, enjoy the contact with them, understand their financial realities and their reluctance to dust until moving out day. Very few successful student landlords need agents. Huge numbers of landlords enjoy modest contact with their tenants. Many want to do a good job and take their responsibilities very seriously. These buildings are, after all, seriously expensive assets that must earn their keep. And *no* independent landlord wants to have empty buildings so they tend to look after their tenants – because that's how they earn their money. However, beware the landlord who talks too much and listens too little when you first meet them. They won't change.

### But isn't an agency just more competent?

I couldn't possibly say – you tell me.

### WARNING ANECDOTES

One landlord local to me rang, almost hysterical, during local flash floods. Her mother's beautiful home was let out via a very reputable agency which had just admitted that they'd handed over every single key for the rental to the tenants and hadn't thought to keep one for emergencies. Meanwhile, our panicky caller had visited and peered through the windows. Her mother's antique furniture was bobbing around in 18 inches of flood water. We advised her to call the fire brigade, who promptly broke down the front door. Unfortunately, the conscientious tenant had locked every single internal door with the only set of keys and gone to Hong Kong for Christmas. Lots more broken doors.

And a nightmare that should never have arisen if management had ensured they could access the building in cases of emergency to protect their client's property.

In a separate incident, imagine my surprise that a leading agency manager admitted that more than half their properties didn't have gas safety certificates because, again, they'd given all the keys to tenants, most of whom were reluctant to take a day off work to allow gas safety engineers to do their job.

---

*Tip* For safety checks and essential maintenance, make sure that your agent does have a spare key. You shouldn't have to lose a day's pay for work like safety checks. However tenants taking on property when management issues like these are so slack can have trouble on their hands. Always try to rent from someone who seems competent about the whole process. There's far more to letting property than simply snatching the money; with it comes a responsibility for the welfare and wellbeing of your tenants.

---

Property management with tenants in place requires co-operation between parties. You want to be safe and it's the management's responsibility to see that you are. I can't imagine a single independent landlord handing over every key to their precious investment without retaining an emergency only spare. But don't allow your landlord to wander willy nilly through your life just because they have a key. If they begin doing so, politely but firmly tell them that you have a right to 24 hours' written notice when they need to come inside and that they need a reason to disturb your privacy. They may not like it – but they certainly can't argue with it.

## What costs can I expect to pay?

Taking on strangers to let them live (guaranteed for six months minimum) does require some background checks that the tenant is expected to pay for to validate their suitability. Expect charges for:

■ **References**.

■ **Parental guarantor forms** if required.

■ **Credit checks and bank and employer references**. Agencies charge all kinds of fees. As these numbers begin to mount up, agents often throw in other 'unexpected fees', which can again amount to considerable sums of money.
   – **Check-in costs**.
   – **Inventory fees**.
   – **Lease** *signing* **fees**.

On and on goes the list of charges that a tenant is expected to meet with a smile.

> So, if you do decide to use agents, be certain that you have a written list of *all their charges* upfront and long before you start looking at any specific property on their books. And *take a good look* at that lengthy contract you'll be required to sign.

Buried in the small print can be a variety of other hidden goodies for agents. Watch out for things you're signing up to pay for! Add them up. If you don't want or can't afford these, try finding a decent private landlord. There are thousands and thousands of them. And again, ask even the friendliest of landlords what up front fees there will be to move in.

### The reference game

**WARNING ANECDOTE**

Some agents have a number of tenants, or groups of tenants, all interested in renting one particular property. This is understandably more likely the more appealing the property. Do make sure that you are not in some kind of race, where several groups of potential tenants are all being charged for references, but where only one group can, naturally enough, ever be successful. Ask the agent to confirm – before you agree to pay up – if anyone else is being considered for the same property and if they are already taking up references on anyone else's behalf. Several interested groups all being multi-referenced simultaneously at £35 each applicant can be very profitable for agencies and a costly mistake for the disappointed majority who all end up out of luck and pocket.

## Sealed bids

### WARNING ANECDOTE

Agents with their eye on the main chance have decided that sealed bids is the way forward when several tenants want a particular unit. Be very, very careful. Raising your rent voluntarily by £30/£40/£50 per week soon mounts up and tenants can easily over-extend themselves in a flash of enthusiasm they may well regret. In large cities there is *always* something else that fits your budget – look for fixed priced units that match your bank balance. This kind of phenomenon is part and parcel of the current London property hype that drives prices relentlessly higher in some form of insanity, disconnected from most tenants' reality. It's a big boys' game for city traders looking for something in quite specific small areas with prestigious addresses, not something that the majority of tenants should even entertain. If asked for a sealed bid, do your sums very carefully before getting involved with this kind of 'arrangement'. It suits agents and a minority of landlords, not tenants.

## That costly lease renewal

After your first fixed term comes to an end and, if you're happy to stay in the unit, if the agent tries to insist that you sign up for a whole new lease or tries charging you for a **lease extension** or some other such thing, when there are no changes being made to the terms (say a rent increase), try explaining to them that by simply staying put and paying the rent you're quite happy to let your lease become a **statutory periodic tenancy** without any more paperwork, thank you very much all the same (all explained in more detail later in Lesson 7 on leases). It saves committing you to a whole full six months' liability, while still safeguarding both your and your landlord's interests nicely. It's the perfect solution that agents don't suggest because they're used to simply charging and no one asking why – let alone what legal necessity any of this has, beyond being another fee generator.

Get yourself a copy of the government's fabulous free booklet called the Assured and Assured Shorthold Tenancies: A guide for tenants. Call 0870 1226 236 and ask for one, the product code is 97 HC 228C. Better still, copy in hand, look up the Statutory Periodic page 19 and show it to your landlord/agent. Give it a shot. It may even save you some fees.

## Maintaining good relationships

### Jaw jaw is better than war war

Whoever you rent from, always do your best to establish some kind of rapport. Discussion is always better than confrontation. For those of you renting through agents remember that the agency may well privately agree with your point of view, however they are employed by the landlord and a landlord veto on repairs stops any agency dead in its tracks.

### Letting agency organisations

Some letting agents have joined voluntary associations. Most haven't. The lettings industry is sadly without a meaningful regulator or universal rules, but if your agent is a member of any voluntary group and you are having problems, they *may* be able to advise you although they won't directly intervene on your behalf.

### Behind the scenes relationships

Unbeknown to tenants, landlords and agents are often in major dispute behind the scenes about how many deductions are to be made from your deposit (all this will soon be ironed out as landlords and agents are obliged to safeguard deposits after April 2007). Agencies can find that, while they may think that a full deposit return is due, the landlord is adamantly demanding deductions. As stated before, agents are employed by landlords, not tenants. Many agents have given a written undertaking to their landlords that they will not release deposit refunds without the landlord's consent (again due to change soon but still in existence on current deposits which will hang over for quite some time). However, these kinds of demands from landlords can place agents in very tricky positions.

# And finally

Work out a realistic budget: how much for this, for that, for the other, etc. Ask your questions, reasonable people will understand that you're being sensible.

---

Take it from me – the *one* thing a decent landlord is looking hard to find is a sensible tenant, who budgets carefully.

---

Unreasonable/unrealistic/uninformed people on either side of the contract make renting/letting harder work than anyone wants or needs.

## Then it's down to you

Don't expect to be mollycoddled through life just because you're paying rent – even quite a lot of it. In a famous legal judgment Lord Denning set the benchmark when he ruled that *a tenant must do the little things around the place that a tenant ought reasonably to do*. So, screw the door handle back on yourself if it's worked itself a bit loose. Don't call every time a light bulb or a fuse blows. And remember, fridges stop working if you never defrost them, washing machines won't spin if the filter's blocked up with loose change and dishwashers won't leave your dishes shiny if you never clean them out.

If your landlord/agent refuses to carry out essential repairs, after a couple of prompting calls write to them, send your concerns recorded delivery, keep the postal slip and keep a copy for your records. Landlords are often busy people so they don't jump every time someone calls over something like a dripping tap. However, major repairs like heating failure should be under serious landlord/agent review within 24 hours. Likewise, if your agent is being chary about fixing that boiler – ring twice then write and complain formally. It may not work, but it's the best shot I can give you in a very uneven service like rentals. Like it or not, *you* are the only quality control in the rental market.

# Lesson 6

# Living as a tenant

So many areas of dispute between landlords and tenants arise because of simple misunderstandings. Although much of this has been covered in bits elsewhere, this is a chance to take the concept of being a tenant down in one big gulp. Tenants are often genuinely unsure about their areas of responsibility. This section is designed to help you understand your status as a tenant better, by explaining in simple terms what you can expect from your landlord/agent, and what he/she can expect from you.

Living as a tenant is quite different from, say, living at home. It is also very different from living in any property as an owner-occupier. You have a formal contract, which governs your behaviour and the manner in which you live, and you really do have to abide by it if you want your tenancy to be trouble-free – let alone be extended. Here, there's no one else to clean up after you, and you will be charged if you leave a mess behind when you leave. In this arrangement, no one will good-humouredly accept a broken chair-leg, or a burn mark from the iron on the dining-room table. Whatever damage is caused by you, however small, you will be billed the full commercial rate for its repair. The cost of these repairs can be very surprising, especially to those of you with 'handy' parents.

> You are not free to redecorate without consent, and if you do need consent for *anything*, especially if you are dealing with any third party, you need it in writing.

## Responsibility for damages

### *From the beginning*

Let us start with simple things first. If you break anything, you will need to pay for its replacement. You may alternatively be asked to replace it yourself. Do make sure that you are replacing like with like. Do not replace a beautiful mirror with a cheap alternative, or a couple of mirror tiles. It will not be accepted on final inspection. Conversely, dispute demands for a beautiful mirror, if the one you broke was a mottled old thing. It is also best not to throw away the broken bits of anything away, until you are sure that your landlord or agent is satisfied with the replacement you are suggesting, because you will have a terrible problem proving the likely value of anything you tossed in the bin.

### When things get trickier

The fundamental requirement of your lease is that you return the property to the landlord in the same condition as when you moved in. With a broken item, it is relatively easy to sort out. Things can get a bit more complicated when responsibility is a little blurred. If for example the main drain blocks, and sewage is seeping odiously around the back door, the landlord or agent needs to be informed so that they can initiate repairs. If it is a problem with the condition of the drains, that is the landlord's responsibility. If however you have blocked the pipe by stuffing disposable nappies down it all week, the cost of unblocking and clean-up will be yours, even if the landlord or agent insists on making all the necessary arrangements.

### Insurance

Never assume that your landlord's insurance will cover your own negligence. Many insurers will pay out to the landlord, and then seek to recover their costs from the responsible party. It is no good therefore setting the chip pan alight, and expecting someone else to pay for your own carelessness. Landlords will only insure their building and their own contents. Tenants must insure their own personal belongings. This can sometimes be harder than it should be. If you really can't find an insurer willing to cover your things, try adding them as additional cover to your parents' or any responsible adult's policy on a declared 'away from home' status – that sometimes works. Students can always get cover via their student union.

### Liability for conduct

As the tenant, you are also liable for the conduct of anyone else you invite into your landlord's property. Damage during parties is a classic example. If there is damage caused, the costs will be down to you. Additionally, you are expected to behave 'in a tenant-like manner', and you must take sensible precautions against damage. Some landlords may ask you to sign an additional list of terms, or may have a very comprehensive lease drawn up with specific requirements and responsibilities for their tenants. These might include things like 'to play music, TV, etc with due consideration for other residents', or 'to leave heating on during any winter periods when the tenant is absent from the building for more than 24 hours'.

If you can't satisfy the terms, don't sign it. Never sign and then assume that ignoring terms will work. It won't. And legal grounds exist for landlords to ask for very rapid eviction if you:

■ persistently invite troublemakers to your home
■ allow it to be used to deal drugs or for any illegal activity.

The old school of absent landlord who didn't give a damn has thankfully been replaced by a huge number of very interested investors who have paid vast sums of money for rental property. And believe me – they *do* give a damn! Heaven be praised for progress.

---

### WARNING ANECDOTE

An apparently responsible tenant left his rented house in Macclesfield to visit his parents in Hampshire, and, in an attempt to economise, turned off the central heating boiler and went home for ten days. A severe cold snap burst the mains water supply pipe in the roof. Over the next several days, tens of thousands of gallons of water coursed through the empty building, drawing the attention of the neighbours only when a glassy puddle decorated the front step. By the time the management was called, every ceiling in the building was down, and not one item of contents salvageable. Both landlord and tenant lost everything they owned. The landlord was insured, the tenant had economised on insurance. The tenant needed rehousing for two months until the property had been repaired. Unsurprisingly, he was not offered an extension to his fixed term.

### On the other hand

There are some circumstances in which the condition of the building adversely affects tenants. Lots of cheaper housing has a condensation problem, and condensation is a major cause of mould. This can grow on one's clothes, which are ruined, and destroy your personal possessions. This problem is one which is usually the responsibility of the landlord. In these circumstances tenants can act against the landlord, if they are willing to do so. Damp and mould are associated with ill health, and some tenants have successfully, with the help of legal advisors, sued landlords.

If only possessions are affected, write to your landlord with a list of damaged goods, and if all else fails, sue for their replacement through the Small Claims Court, even after your tenancy has ended, if they did not respond to your letters while you lived there. However, if the building was perfectly dry when you moved in, and you have never opened a window for ventilation as the washer boiled away – or worse, blocked fitted ventilation grilles, expect comeback from the landlord if you have introduced a major problem.

Even in prestigious properties things can go awry. Here, lavish features or fittings included in the rent must work, and continue to work if they are included in the rent. If repairs are slow, hustle. Believe me, if your rent is slow you will be hustled!

## Can the landlord visit the property while I am a tenant?

Landlords do have a statutory right (under the 1988 Act) to enter the property at reasonable times of the day to carry out repairs, or to inspect the condition of their property. However, unless an emergency as urgent as the last anecdote exists, they should always give you 24 hours' notice in writing.

These landlords' rights of entry don't allow them to come and go as they please. Landlords need to notify you formally that they are exercising their rights of entry and have good reason for doing so. They may need to carry out works. Alternatively, they may wish to carry out, say, a quarterly inspection of the condition of their property.

This must not deteriorate into a series of unnecessary calls. As a tenant you are buying with your rent the 'right to quiet enjoyment'. The property you are renting is your home, and good landlords and agents will automatically respect this. Of course, repeated unnecessary calls are a subtle form of harassment – read the Lesson and take some advice about endless 'social' calls.

### When property is rented while up for sale

Some tenants find that they are living in property that is simultaneously up for sale. In these instances tenants are entitled to the same notice of intention to enter as in any other circumstances. Estate agents are still bound to offer tenants in buildings they are trying to sell a right of 'quiet enjoyment' and need to write to tenants, giving at least 24 hours' notice that they will be arriving with a potential purchaser for a property viewing.

## Using your charms

Some of the most useful advice that this author can give about problem-solving during tenancies is to develop the best working relationship you can with your landlord or agent. This industry is bedevilled by the conflicting histories of Rachman versus the Tenant from Hell, and if you're too young to know who Rachman was, he's now in the *Oxford Dictionary*, look him up. Interesting guy.

All too often, either landlord or tenant have had previous serious problems which prejudice their views of one another. The landlord who seems to have rule after rule may have had a previous very bad experience. There are awful tenants as well as awful landlords. Landlords do see their fair share of irresponsible conduct, and can get very frustrated dealing with the irresponsibility of this tiny minority.

**WARNING ANECDOTE**

A landlord, looking for a small set of drawers for a flat, called by a secondhand dealer he knew. Seeing a small chest he liked, he noticed other items which also looked good ... and rather familiar. Closer inspection revealed the entire contents of one of his own properties on display. Everything was there, from the carpets to the lightshades. Before moving out, the tenant had sold the entire contents of his landlord's flat to a dealer for a small sum of money. Landlords, as well as tenants, do have their problems.

So wherever possible aim to be on decent, working terms with whoever is managing your property. Tenants renting property through agents can, in many ways, have a quite different set of problems to tenants dealing directly with their own landlord. Agencies act as 'brokers' between landlords and tenants, drawing money for their role as go-between. Although this sometimes works well, too often tenants find it is used as an excuse for failure to manage the property well. 'We still haven't heard back from the landlord' is not much consolation if you're waiting for an essential repair. It can however work equally badly for the unsuspecting landlord sometimes.

### WARNING ANECDOTE

A tenant took a pleasant property with no apparent problems. A couple of days later he called the agency, complaining about slugs in the kitchen. Billing the landlord by the hour (£50ph + VAT to be precise) the agency sent out a maintenance man, who found one slug trail on the doormat. He inspected, and reported back. Numerous phone calls and much abuse followed, the agents responding with seven call-outs, and the laying of slug pellets, traps and salt, all being billed by the hour to the unsuspecting landlord in the tenant's first month. Apparently one particularly resolute slug had decided that this was going to be his nocturnal route whatever anyone else thought! In this case, the unreasonable demands of the tenant rather than the landlord resulted in a large deduction from the landlord's revenue. Being a tenant doesn't absolve you from all normal domestic tasks. Including relocating a determined but harmless slug.

## Subletting

Most assured shorthold leases specifically exclude subletting without consent. This is considered as quite a serious breach of terms by most landlords. If you want a partner to move in, most landlords or agents will not object, so long as the partner's name is put on the lease and normal checks stack up. However, expect this situation to become much tighter as new safety legislation (April 2007) requires many landlords with more than two tenants to be licensed; a costly and bureaucratic process that many landlords with smaller units will quite reasonably seek to avoid.

## Rental payments

You *must* pay your rent on time, and in the manner agreed with your landlord. Landlords and agents are running businesses and the sole reason that you live in their properties is for the money that you generate. Excuses, late payments and insufficient payments are simply unacceptable.

There may in some instances be a genuine reason (as opposed to a lame excuse) why your rent will not be available. If this happens, get on the phone and discuss it immediately with whoever manages your property. It is silly and irresponsible to not say anything, to go out when the collection is due, or just to not have sufficient funds to cover that direct debit. Rubber cheques are particularly unpopular with owners/agents.

Nor do you have the right (except in some very rare cases for which you would need *serious* legal advice) to withhold payments because, in your opinion, the landlord or agent haven't fulfilled some obligation. The matters are separate, and need to be dealt with separately. If you have a case (fair or otherwise) against your landlord, you cannot deduct your own opinion of its value from rent. Indeed, rent comes before all other considerations. Before Friday night's blowout. Or the phone bill. Rent keeps the roof over your head. After all, 20 Benson & Hedges will only keep your fingers warm, and not even that much if it's raining.

### The consequences of regularly late rent

A legal ground for your landlord to use for possession is that you have been persistently late paying your rent. Proof of current arrears is not always required. The payment record itself can be considered if you really irritate your landlord enough that he heads for court.

> If you pay your rent weekly you are legally entitled to a rent book, which your landlord needs to sign.

If they don't know where to get one, buy one yourself from any large stationers.

If you pay by cash, ask for and save all receipts as proof of payment. Always ask when your tenancy is starting and, if the rent is to be collected, by whom. Tenants renting low cost weekly rent 'in cash please' are most vulnerable to shenanigans. Be certain that you don't pay one person, not get a receipt, and then find that another, quite different person calls later, still expecting to be paid.

### WARNING ANECDOTE

Before you imagine that something like this couldn't possibly happen, let me assure you that it has. Student tenants in Birmingham paid one of the brothers in a family their rent (in cash...no receipt), only to find the brother whom they normally paid arrived an hour later for the rent! It can sometimes be quite difficult to placate an aggressive landlord, and they do exist. This case made the national press and caused much amusement. I daresay the frightened tenants didn't find it much of a hoot at all.

# Lesson 7

# Leases

Here things can sound a bit technical but I'll do my best to make it as clear as I can. Nevertheless – with money like this changing hands – you owe it to yourself to learn some quite specific things. Landlord–tenant law is immense, but assured shorthold tenancies only utilise a small core of this existing legislation. You only need to know about the parts of them that affect you and how you'll live. Those of you with more appetite for detail can find unlimited browsing resources online.

So let's start with the absolute basics. And let's keep things simple. Almost every tenancy now available to you will be one type or another of assured shorthold tenancy. They are the current currency that keeps investment pouring into the rental market.

## What is a lease?

It's a contract. Pure and simple. It can be anything from four pages long to 30 plus pages of close typed script in size 8 font. However impenetrable, always insist on taking the time to read your lease. Once you've signed it, you're bound by it. And by all those itty bitty things hidden in sub clause 2a) iv – or whatever. If you don't want to sign it, there's no compulsion.

So read leases and make decisions about what you want or don't. You are half of this contract – in fact you're the one with the money everyone wants – so learn how to make a deal. Good lettings/rentals are 'win win' situations, where both sides get a degree of what they want from contracts.

### Private landlords

The majority of private landlords buy leases from legal suppliers like Oyez. They are cheap, simple to understand, comply with fair contract terms and legally enforceable. They don't contain any hidden clauses and everything in them complies with the terms of the relevant housing legislation. They rarely included clauses allowing non-negotiable rent increases. We use them because our tenants find them straightforward and so do we.

### Agents

The majority of agents have their own leases drawn up by in-house legal services. Many have inbuilt fees, which can be demanded and many incorporate annual rent increases, which are not negotiable if signed by tenants. Ask for time to read through these leases – however long they are – and insist that anything you don't understand is explained. Because agencies rely on volume with many properties, many tenants and of course lots of itsy bitsy charges that no one mentions out loud, make it your job to read what you're agreeing to *before* you sign any lease.

### But I don't have a lease!

Although it's unwise, some landlords still let out property without paperwork. However by handing over money each week/month, a contract is still created – paperwork or not. So you do have a lease. It's an unwritten lease. And, so long as you moved in after 1997 it's almost without exception an assured shorthold lease. With that contract, however informal and unclear, come some rights for tenants (landlords too). You are legally entitled to certain information in writing: start dates, the amount of rent payable and when to pay it. However, like everything else to do with rentals, some landlords comply with nothing. Nevertheless, you're still legally entitled to that six months' initial security, just like all other similar tenants. Maybe your landlord simply doesn't know – or doesn't *want* to know that – but that's the legal position. With or without words a contract with rights on both sides exists.

> Any tenancy that began after 28 February 1997 is automatically an assured shorthold tenancy unless something else, quite specific and in writing, overrides this fact or if it's a (rare) precluded situation.

All these exceptions and much more are in Appendix A of the government's essential booklet that I keep mentioning: Assured and Assured Shorthold Tenancies: A guide for tenants – product code 97 HC 228C. Call 0870 1226 236 – they're free, a mere phone call away. They're also an absolute godsend to tenants trying to deal with landlords/agents who refuse to believe that you have a point to make *that's valid*. So get one of these booklets. And wield it wherever necessary when management is being unreasonable.

## Assured shorthold leases

Assured shorthold leases *must* comply with the housing legislation.

Like it or not, no landlord or agent can insert things into leases that conflict with the original or revised legislation (1988/1996). Sounds like gobbledygook? Well, let me give you an example. By law, landlords need to give their tenants two months' written notice that they need to leave, to exercise their shorthold rights. That's it, the housing legislation can't be altered, no matter what's been sneaked into the lease to shorten that notice period to one month – two months' notice it is (unless your landlord is acting on a lease breach through court).

### Pre-1997 tenants

Tenants who have lived in their units since before 28 Feb 1997 *must* read this lesson thoroughly. Many tenancies were incorrectly created before this date and a large number of tenancies with unlimited security of tenure (unless lease terms are breached) were created. Many may still exist today.

In plain English, if you have an *old tenancy*, your landlord or agent *may* have accidentally given you a lease that can't be terminated unless you breach the major lease terms. They lost their guaranteed rights to possession that come with shortholds by failing to set up the contract properly.

Recognising what had happened the government changed the law in 1996 so this can no longer happen. Assured shorthold leases no longer require advance paperwork.

As for the rest of you in the here and now, these are the two most widely used types of assured shorthold leases you're likely to be offered:

- fixed term
- periodic or contractual period

and are outlined below.

## Fixed term tenancy

The most popular type by a mile is the fixed term tenancy. This means, in a nutshell, that a specific length of time will be offered for the lease to run initially. This is usually six months, but can be longer/shorter. Six months is popular because it offers maximum *mutual* benefits, hence its huge popularity. *Look on it as a trial run for both parties*. Beyond that there are simple ways to stay put. Assured shortholds can and do run for years – even when they started out with an initial six-month fixed term.

During that fixed term, tenants enjoy a relative period of security. If the initial fixed term offered is, say, a year, then your period of security and rental liability becomes a whole year long. Assured shortholds restrict a landlord's/agent's options for obtaining a 'no fault' guaranteed possession order through the courts until the initial fixed term (or six months) expires, but remain hugely popular because they suit a wide range of circumstances. Also remember that, just as every tenant who hopes their new rental will be a fresh start, every successful landlord is an optimist. We're not looking for reasons to kick you out from day one, but always hope this new tenancy will be trouble free, long term and, of course, profitable.

> Longer doesn't necessarily mean better.

What you gain on the roundabouts you can lose on the swings with fixed terms.

Here's a thought to consider. Signing up for anything beyond the normal six months ties both parties into longer obligations to each other. You may have just found a perfect agent, a perfect land-lord...but on the other hand... So six months is also a fairly decent length of time to test out your own side of the tenancy.

Many agents try to insist that their tenants sign up for an initial fixed term of a whole year from the outset. Again, these things remain in your hands. No one can force you to sign a lease that you don't like the terms of. If you don't want what's being offered, then either negotiate or find an alternative unit with terms that you prefer. A modern landlord/agent with a mid-range property is no longer offering a rarity. Many areas have more property than tenants. So never let management bully you into accepting what's best for them. Learn to look out for you.

> Double the security = double the liability.

### Balancing the pros and cons on fixed terms

It's a tricky balancing act, but try to work these fixed terms to your advantage if you can (it isn't always easy though, some landlords/agents have very resolute policies on these matters). Students for example might do well to *try* negotiating a nine-month lease for their academic year. Many agents will refuse longer initial fixed terms than six months, simply because insisting on a shorter lease gives them the opportunity to offer either a whole new lease or some other dandy thing that agents call a **lease extension fee** – and again charge you for the privilege of staying on a while longer. Nice work if you can get it.

### Final clarification

Because this is the most likely option you'll get as a modern tenant, let's run through it again.

- This fixed term is the legal length of time that ties you and your landlord/agent together into a binding contract.

- You agree to pay rent for the whole of that time and keep the lease terms, in return for which you get some security of tenure.

■ The longer the fixed term, the longer your security *and* the length of time that you're legally responsible for the rent.

■ The shorter the fixed term the shorter your rent obligations *and* your greatest level of security.

■ If you want to leave before your fixed term expires, unless your landlord agrees to end your tenancy (and a surprising number of independent landlords will if, say, work demands a relocation that's beyond your control), you will remain liable for the rent for the remainder of that agreed fixed term – unless or until your landlord/agent finds a suitable replacement tenant.

## Periodic or contractual period tenancy

Assured shorthold leases can also be run as periodic or contractual periodic tenancies (which don't have any fixed term). Basically, these leases run on a month by month basis, meaning that tenants aren't contractually bound into them from the start for any fixed period of time. Meaning also that these types of leases are *rare*. Tenants who don't have fixed terms still enjoy that same six months relative security before the landlord has any guarantee of possession. Therefore these arrangements simply don't balance up. Tenants get security of tenure for six months, while landlords don't get an undertaking on rent for the same period of time. Periodic tenancies give landlord/agent a slightly wider range of options on possession at an earlier stage. They suit (in some cases) tenants who have no intention of staying long – but every time the landlord agrees to this, s/he's running a risk on guaranteed possession without guaranteed rent for the same timeframe. This tends to be a 'top end' option – used for the business classes rather than the majority of tenants who are looking for homes.

## What happens at the end of the initial fixed term?

As usual, one of several things can happen. These are the most likely scenarios, assuming that you are happy to stay on and your landlord/agent has no concern about you doing so.

## *Option 1*

Your landlord/agent approaches you and offers another brand new lease with another fixed term. This ties both of you back to broadly where you started. Landlords can't get guaranteed possession until a new fixed term (or another six months) has expired and tenants are obliged to pay rent for another whole fixed term.

Sometimes it's done this way to incorporate a change in terms that wasn't written into the old lease. For example a rent increase will appear with the new lease. It's *always* up to you as a tenant to decide whether or not to agree to sign a new lease. Of course, declining new terms means finding somewhere else to live. Try negotiating on unexpected rent increases, especially where they come along in under a year. Good tenants with good track records can often trigger a change of heart. But if the management insists that new terms are the only ones on offer you either accept and sign or give notice to leave and find somewhere else.

## *Option 2*

Nothing happens. You continue paying your rent and the landlord continues accepting it. Then, without any further commitments, undertakings or paperwork, the landlord reaches that secure place, beyond the fixed term where they can obtain guaranteed possession if things go pear shaped – and *tenants* don't have to commit for another whole fixed term.

This type of arrangement is called a **statutory periodic tenancy**. It works brilliantly for many landlords and tenants because it offers such great flexibility. It's rarer in agency lettings because, frankly, there's no paperwork that agents can charge for. Under a statutory periodic, landlords and tenants are each able to give notice whenever they choose – so long as they observe the specific rules on giving notice to quit. One of my assured shorthold tenants stayed on for 13 years without ever needing a new lease.

## *Option 3*

One or other of you decides to call it a day. In that case, landlords or tenants must give written notice to close down the tenancy.

There are other variations on this theme, but in the overwhelming majority of cases one of the above will happen.

### Giving notice to leave

Letting people know your intentions in writing is essential. Don't imagine that your landlord/agent will somehow just guess that you intend leaving at the end of your fixed term. On the contrary, unless they hear from you, they'll assume that you want to stay on. You must tell them that you intend leaving in writing – at least one month beforehand. So, if you intend leaving at the end of a six-month fixed term, write and inform your landlord that you will be leaving then, no later than five months into your lease.

## What you need to know about leases

> Leases are important legal documents.

- They must be signed by both landlord and tenant (or agent).
- They must be witnessed and dated to be valid.
- The landlord/agent has a copy, you have an identical copy.
- You are legally obliged to observe all the terms of the lease you have signed, unless something has been added which is not acceptable in law (if you've been asked to sign something that is obviously weighted against you, get your local housing officer or Citizen's Advice Bureau to check it out).

### Security of tenure really matters

Good tenants who pay their rent on time, look after the unit and don't cause damage (or hassle the landlord with an endless stream of daft demands) have all the security they'll usually ever need, so don't get too hooked up on lengthy fixed terms. Landlords/agents want tenants in place and paying rent. That security aspect is already largely in your own hands and it's called good tenant conduct.

> Good tenants are secure because they are desirable.

Landlords/agents only bother with all the hassle and costs of forcing out troublesome tenants in the most unusual of circumstances. Abide by your lease and you'll become a welcome partner in what can often become a lengthy business partnership.

### Break clauses

Sometimes, before agreeing to rent a property for a fixed period of time, a tenant will ask for a **break clause** to be inserted. These give an opportunity for a tenant to leave on a certain date, agreed mutually before the tenancy begins, written into the lease and usually mid-way through at, say, three months. They are not standard clauses, and will certainly not be found in a standard lease. They are quite common in more expensive units, and almost standard in company lettings. Seek specialist advice, or use a very reputable agency if you are looking for this type of arrangement.

### A reality check for many tenants on tight budgets

No matter how well informed they are, tenants can and do *still* find themselves in property which is unfit to live in, or positively unsafe. The huge demand, particularly in university towns, and now some very expensive cities (especially in the south east) has caused a real shortage of safe, *affordable* accommodation. If you have been fortunate/ determined enough to obtain a lease from your landlord/agent, which covers *the full period* you wish to live there under the first fixed term, you do have the relatively safe option of asking your local environmental health department to inspect, and at least check if you are covered under new and existing safety laws.

Why? Because, no matter what the outcome, you can't lose your home until the fixed term has expired unless you break a lease term.

If however you have only been able to obtain a 'fix' of six months when perhaps you need nine to complete your course, or you have a year's short-term employment contract and a six month fixed term, you run the genuine risk of being asked to leave if you complain at all. Landlords running unsafe multi-let properties can take a very dim view of being 'reported to the council'.

Meanwhile all too often, tenants dependent on lease extensions are too afraid to complain about anything at all. It can take a brave person indeed to insist to some of the more assertive landlords that, as tenants, they enjoy certain rights, however limited.

■ Being prepared before you become a tenant is the best safeguard you can have.

■ Being aware if you already are a tenant is the second best.

Never forget, your lease does offer you some safeguards, if you know where to find them. While some landlords can become a bit belligerent, they too are bound by the contracts they entered into when they took your rent. And there are a surprising number of organisations out there to help you through difficult times.

### Does it matter when my lease began?

It can be crucial! Following the introduction of assured shorthold tenancies in 1988, many landlords and some agents did not comply with the strict requirement to serve the tenant with a Section 20 notice advising them that the tenancy was an assured shorthold. Despite everyone signing documents titled 'assured shorthold tenancies', *unless the Section 20 Notice that the tenancy was an assured shorthold was served before the tenancy agreement was signed*, the tenancy created was in fact a straightforward assured tenancy, with extensive security of tenure inadvertently given to the tenants, often without either party realising what they had accidentally created – let alone just been handed on a golden plate.

Recognising the problem, revisions were put in place for *all tenancies starting on or after 28 February 1997,* and now, unless otherwise quite specifically stated in writing, all tenancies (within the framework – i.e. the overwhelming majority) are automatically assured *shorthold* tenancies.

## Licenses

There is a huge difference between a tenancy and a licence to occupy part of the landlord's home. Where tenancies offer limited security, licences offer virtually none. Nevertheless, they can and do work really well and continue to be tremendously popular. How you *occupy* determines whether or not you're a tenant or a licensee. No landlord who lives elsewhere (i.e. in a nice safe house up the hill) can offer a license and it be genuine. These arrangements exist for **resident landlords** who live in the same building as their licensees.

| To be a tenant, you must have some exclusivity in the unit. |
| --- |

Genuine licensees have living arrangements where their landlord has specified they need unrestricted access to every room in their property, for services like weekly cleaning and who live alongside their paying occupants.

Although not strictly in the remit of this guide, because situations overlap so much I shall give some general information on licensing/lodging arrangements. This is an increasing rather than decreasing phenomenon. Many people with hefty mortgages take in someone to help with costs. In order to make this work, landlords can't be expected to have someone whose lifestyle is inconvenient claiming security of tenure for months on end – it's just too invasive. Most licences can legitimately be closed down by landlords within a week.

### WARNING ANECDOTE

To tide over a homeowner with a huge mortgage, the owner took in two lodgers to help with costs until a buyer could be found. One was fine – unobtrusive, polite and friendly. The second was a 'student' whose parents paid his costs very erratically. Plus this guy simply never left the flat at all. Waking mid-afternoon he then simply dominated the living room and integral kitchen, leaving a trail of cookery devastation, loud music, TV playing 24/7 and liked to use the landlord's free internet service to access porn sites. Matters finally came to a head when the owner returned home to find a large, unmentioned party in full swing. Of course the lodger had to leave and he did. But landlords offering a limited right to occupy expect what is still their own home to be treated with respect by what are, in effect, paying guests.

There's rarely anything much by way of paperwork with these arrangements, but they work. Lodgers or licensees live in happy coincidence with landlords up and down the country. Many live there during the week and return to family homes at weekends. Many share meals with families. It can be an extraordinarily expedient way to live for lots of people. What it doesn't offer is much security.

### Could my licence actually be a lease?

Possibly. Many people bought up large properties when prices were cheap and still offer them out for rent. They don't live on the premises – many only visit to collect rent. Facilities like kitchens or bathrooms are shared. Yet they continue to insist to tenants that they are offering licenses with no security.

> Unless you have a resident landlord with unrestricted access, you cannot be offered a genuine licence. These landlords are creating tenancies, whatever they claim.

Anyone asked to leave arrangements like this at short notice should quibble. You are probably a tenant – with the security that offers – whatever your landlord insists. Calling by each week to collect rent and to throw a few eggs and bread in the fridge doesn't cut it. Licences are actually quite hard to create and it takes more than the ingredients for eggs on toast to remove someone's genuine security.

If the landlord doesn't live in the same building (and I don't mean a separate flat downstairs either) what matters in law is what is happening on the ground. By paying anyone money for accommodation you are creating either a licence or a tenancy. Indeed, if a document claims one arrangement, but how you *live* contradicts that paperwork, then court decisions will be based on how you live, not what a piece of paper pretends to have offered. Even when no paper changes hands, again the oral tenancy may apply.

### Has a tenancy been created?

If your landlord doesn't live on the premises, or owns a number of buildings filled with occupants, as is common, she or he will very often have *offered* a licence or lodgings, but may easily have inadvertently *created* a tenancy. This may be a genuine lack of knowledge on their part, or a deliberate attempt to reduce your rights. If you have exclusive use of any part of any property, for example, your own room that no one else enters, or if you have been given any specific length of time which you can occupy the building, you are very much more likely to have a tenancy than a licence.

It may be that when you came to view the room the 'landlord' said something along the lines of, 'oh, I don't bother with all that paperwork stuff. Everyone here gets along fine. No need to make anything too official. If people aren't happy, they just move on.' It's like buying a car without a log book. If you still want that room, because you like it, or because it's cheap, take it by all means. But once you are settled, quietly find out where you stand legally.

**If your landlord insists that you have a licence not a tenancy**, ask yourself the following questions.

- Do you occupy part of a converted house, e.g. a flat or bed-sit, within a building where your landlord or another member of his family lives? This may be a licence.

- Do you have a fixed term that you are obliged to stay for (e.g. six months? You may well have a tenancy.

- Do you share any facilities with your landlord, for example bathrooms, or kitchens? If so you may have a licence. If your sharing only applies to corridors or entrances, and you have exclusive use of some part of the building, you may have a tenancy.

- Are you provided with any services by your landlord? For example, are they or their staff able to enter your room on a weekly basis to clean? If so, you may have a licence. If, however, you basically look after yourself, and landlords empty the rubbish, or provide clean sheets each week, you *may* have a tenancy.

- Do you have exclusive use of any part of the building, into which no one else ever comes? (Even if your landlord lives downstairs this can offer you slightly more protection.) You may have a tenancy.

Perhaps it is easier to explain in the following way. If you live in a student hall of residence, with cleaning and catering, you usually have a licence. If you live in a hotel where staff clean and cater, you have a licence. Try to apply these criteria to your own circumstances. If they are a close match, and your landlord or a member of their family lives in the same building, you may very well have a genuine licence. This is however one of the most controversial areas of law and if you think that your circumstances don't seem to match these, talk to someone who can advise you. Tenants with little money may even be entitled to Legal Aid.

# And finally

In conclusion it might be added that while no one wants to advise anyone to endlessly confront the management, to offer licences simply to deny people what are already very limited rights is hardly a position anyone should want to encourage. Assured shorthold tenancies offer very considerable safeguards in favour of landlords, but every form of earning one's income carries a small degree of risk and being a landlord is no exception. To offer licences as a device to try removing what little security tenants actually do enjoy may seem to many people (both inside and outside the industry) to be a bit unreasonable.

### About renting

There's still a uniquely UK attitude towards being a tenant that permeates every tier of rentals. A smugness that some acceptable social level is only reached by owning property. The *truth* is that the rentals market is top heavy with highly educated, hard working, intelligent and responsible people, holding down excellent jobs. They pay astonishingly high rents and behave with surprising tolerance towards a management system that often fails to treat them with the respect they're jolly well entitled to.

Some frankly medieval attitudes where landlords/agents try to 'lord it' over tenants (and the 'title' doesn't help much either) should have gone out with tithes. Don't accept patronising attitudes, broken agreements, overcharging, under-servicing or indifference to legitimate requirements or concerns. Tenants are *equal* parties to this legal contract. Tenants are also *customers* not chattels. Without their money, landlords and agents couldn't make it through the shortest fixed term going.

If you are signing a lease on any property here are some sensible tips.

■ Read it – you would be amazed how few people do – and preferably before you sign it!

■ Work out how long you will need to live in the property and try to negotiate the most convenient lease length that you can. Try to maximise the fixed term if you are certain you want to live there for a certain length of time. If you don't think you want to stay long, try to negotiate the shortest fixed term available. If all else fails, try for a break clause.

■ If you only need to rent for three months, try not to take a lease for six; the likelihood is that you will end up paying through the nose for the privilege.

■ If you are being asked to sign a licence agreement, get it checked out at some time. You may have accidentally just been offered a tenancy.

■ Don't sign anything that worries you. Unreasonable clauses need to be deleted, not agreed to and optimistically ignored.

■ Observe all the clauses in the lease you agreed to sign, not just those you like.

■ Keep all your documentation safe.

# Lesson 8

# Understanding your lease

Often the leases that assured shorthold tenants are offered come from standard legal stationers. These are usually obvious, with the name of the legal stationers clearly stated, generally on the back page. Alternatively, you could be presented with a standard lease, prepared by your agent's lawyers – these too will usually be titled. The third alternative is a specific lease on several typed pages, drawn up by a solicitor engaged by the landlord. Often these too will have the name of the firm somewhere obvious at the beginning or the end. Your lease is likely to have a title something like this:

> Tenancy agreement for letting a (furnished/unfurnished) dwelling house on an assured shorthold tenancy under Part 1 of the Housing Act 1988.

## Standard terms

Here is a little exploration of some (but by no means all) of the clauses you may find to give a general feel for what some unfamiliar phrases mean. I have also included details of rent increase mechanisms where they often overlap with leases.

■ **'A term certain of...'** is normally found on a **fixed term** tenancy. The landlord or agent will fill in here six months, or nine months, whatever has been decided. This then is usually the length of your **fixed term**, where you enjoy the greatest security.

Unless you find something specific stating otherwise on your lease, the rent agreed will usually remain for the duration of the fixed term.

■ **Break clauses**, giving either party a right to terminate before the fixed term ends, should be specifically written into leases with dates.

■ **Rent reviews** at (say) six-monthly or yearly intervals can be included in the lease. If they have not been written into the lease, no specific provision has been made for them. Wording might therefore simply be 'the landlord lets, and the tenant takes the property **for the term**, (x) at the rent (x).'

■ **Rents** can be referred to as weekly, monthly or pcm. AST leases usually state when money should be received, each rent period, e.g. each Monday, or every four weeks, or perhaps on the 25th of each calendar month.

■ **If rent increases** can legitimately be automatically raised, some note of when, and how and when rent will be reviewed must be written into your lease.

■ **Landlords/agents wanting to increase rents during fixed terms** must have their tenant's agreement. If the tenant disagrees, the landlord will have to wait until the fixed term ends to begin legal processes for a rent increase.

■ **At the end of fixed terms** landlords are perfectly entitled to propose rent increases – it's up to you whether or not you accept them or decide to move on.

References to **the property** include reference to any **part or parts of** the property, **furniture, fixtures**, etc usually incorporates tenant liability for taking care not to damage the property itself by design (banging those nails into walls!) or neglect, say by not notifying management about the necessity for repairs which damage the building (e.g. leaking pipes) and everything that comes with the property, including everything incorporated on the **inventory/building schedule**.

## Explaining the terms

Some terms are obvious, they cover rent payments, accepting responsibility for gas, electricity, water and sewerage charges, and usually commit you to liability for local authority taxes.

■ Tenants will often see terms like, **yield up the property at the end of the tenancy**, which means, simply, leave and return all keys to the landlord/agent.

■ Some leases have a clause which insists that tenants do nothing which **vitiates insurance**. This means to make invalid, or ineffectual, a landlord's insurance. This might mean bringing in paraffin or other portable heaters, which are prohibited by your landlord's insurers, or messing about with the electrical supply and, say, causing a fire. It could also mean ensuring that the building is kept secure (i.e. locked). These clauses are not always specific, in fact they are meant to be quite wide, to offer some security for the landlord's broad based and considerable investment. You are required as tenants to treat the property with respect and are also expected to look after things like security. Use your common sense and treat the place with as much care as you'd treat your own things and you won't go too far wrong.

■ **Make good pay for or repair or replace** places a responsibility upon tenants to return the property and contents in the same operational and decorative condition provided when you moved in. Usually a statement that **reasonable wear and tear are excepted** appears, meaning that landlords can't charge for routine main-tenance (like replacing old carpets or freshening up decorations which have deteriorated not through abuse, but simply by being in use). In effect, tenants have already compensated the landlord for wear and tear by paying their rent.

### Typical terms

Some leases specifically instruct tenants to return all furniture to the positions they were in on acceptance of the property. There is sometimes a very troublesome lease requirement to wash all linens 'soiled during the tenancy'. It's been deleted from many legal service leases because of unforeseen problems. Where tenants find this they should apply common sense yet again. If you feel it necessary to clean the curtains because you smoke like a chimney, don't put your landlord's expensive drapes through the launderette! Check what is being required, use your common sense or *ask* if you're confused.

■ **No pets** is a very typical restriction. This does include hamsters as well as wolfhounds.

■ Commonly there will be specific lease obligations, for example: **not sublet without landlord/agent consent**, which means don't move someone else in to help pay part of the rent without permission first.

■ **Assign**, means not to move out and give the property to anyone else; or **receive paying guests**, without the landlord's specific written *prior* consent (which means *before* you do it, not afterwards when the landlord/agent finds out).

■ Your use of any rented housing is usually confined specifically to **normal residential use**. You cannot then carry out any business without prior written consent.

■ **Permit the landlord or the landlord's agents** (which can mean the lettings agent, or the landlord's employees for example) **to enter the property to view the condition** is usually accompanied by the condition of **at reasonable hours**. The landlord would usually be expected to give 24 hours' written notice of this date and time.

■ **To enter in case of emergency**, or **reserves right of entry for emergencies**, would reasonably allow a landlord to enter without necessarily being obliged to give notice, if for example there was a serious problem which couldn't wait 24 hours, like a burst pipe. This does not of course cover straightening the curtains, as mentioned previously.

### When you've given notice that you intend leaving

Very commonly the lease will contain a clause which **permits the landlord or their agents to enter and view the property with prospective tenants**. This is usually restricted to **at reasonable hours, within the last 28 days of the tenancy**. As mentioned earlier this does not include turning up unannounced, let alone barging straight in without knocking.

> By observing all the lease requirements, and paying their rent as agreed, the tenant buys *the right to quiet enjoyment*.
> This should be free of all unreasonable interference and interruption from the landlord, or by anyone claiming to, or actually representing them.

# Rent issues

## Can my rent be raised?

Ideally, these issues should have been thrashed out before you signed your contract. However it is really quite rare that tenants ask what rent increases are likely to apply in the future. Perhaps they imagine that if they ask, it will encourage the landlord to start thinking about it too!

Although it isn't particularly good business to begin increasing rent more than once a year, if the management do, and the first fixed term of your tenancy have elapsed, in reality you have the same recurring problem that applies to all the terms of these tenancies. If you challenge it, your landlord still enjoys their guaranteed right of possession with two months' notice.

For many tenants this is therefore theoretical rather than practical information, providing an overview of a few common scenarios. However rents are not house prices – they are fairly stable right now. Expect modest rent increases to occur, but don't accept wild hikes every few months – if they occur, at least look around for a more reasonably priced unit. Keep your eye on the market and always have some idea how much the going rate is locally for property like your own. And don't be afraid to point this out to an overoptimistic landlord/agent. As I said earlier, learn some negotiating skills. Many landlords might suggest a hefty rise, then back off if they think a good tenant will move on.

## Rent increases in fixed term tenancies

Usually the agreement will state that the rent will be fixed for the length of 'the fix' i.e. six, nine or 12 months. It may however 'fix' the rent for six months and then say it will be reviewed at certain intervals. If it does say this, then the rent can go up. If you don't want to agree to pay higher rent in the future, don't sign a lease that commits you to it in advance.

If the landlord or agent wants to increase rent by more than it states in the lease at the end of any fixed term, it becomes your choice to either pay an increased rent or give notice and find somewhere cheaper. Do remember that, as usual, if you decline you are unlikely to have your lease extended.

If you have a fixed term and a lease which does not mention rent increases, your rent can only be raised during the fixed term *if you agree*. If you disagree the landlord has to wait until the end of whatever length 'fix' was on the lease before he can either legally propose a rent increase or act to get the building back.

Your landlord may not propose this method of increase however. Some landlords and agents offer a whole new lease, new fixed term, and a new rent level, every six months. These you must either accept, or decline, then move on, because they are effectively whole new tenancies every time. By offering a whole new secure period, the landlord/agent sometimes feels a rent hike might just be acceptable.

Truthfully, being a tenant in today's climate is tough. Sometimes 'negotiations' are the *last* things that management expects. It's terribly hard to advise anyone how to make these very personal judgement calls about what's fair, what's reasonable. Tenants are invariably on the back foot because they have no meaningful rights once their fixed term has expired. So, you pays your money and you takes your choice. Knowing how costly and inconvenient moving is sometimes makes management push their luck. A new lease with six months more guaranteed security *might* be worth the little extra (especially when faced with the trawl and expense of a move), but don't get fleeced and pay more than a property is worth.

### Rent increases for contractual periodic tenancies

Your landlord should give you at least one month's notice in writing of any proposed increases in rent, usually using a special form called **Landlord's Notice proposing a new rent under an Assured Periodic Tenancy of premises situated in England**. If you receive one of these you have two choices. Either pay the increase, or explain that you cannot afford it. Then either negotiate a rent you can afford, or decide you would rather move. In which case, one or other party serves written notice to quit.

### Rent increases when your lease has become a statutory periodic tenancy

This is once any fixed term has expired unless a new lease has been signed. Again, if your fixed term has expired and you and your landlord want to consider continuing the tenancy, they may want to increase your rent at some time (usually annually). This can be done by using the same form mentioned earlier. Again you have the same choices as previously, and further increases can arise each year the tenancy continues. Again landlords/agents should give you one month's notice of any proposed increase, an opportunity to negotiate/decline. And again, if agreement can't be reached on a higher rent one or other party serves legal notice to quit.

## Licences

Genuine licences are in reality much more flexible arrangements between parties than tenancies. If you have a licence all the terms need to be arranged between yourself and your landlord. Given their almost complete lack of security, landlords are able to ask for rent increases in whatever way is worked out between the parties. Licensees have no formal mechanism for redress. Simply, if the rent reaches a level which you feel is too high, your only genuine strategy is to look for a more reasonably priced unit.

# Lesson 9

# Common tenancy arrangements and responsibilities

## Individual tenancies

Where a single landlord lets a single unit to a single person, life is pretty straightforward. Leases are agreed, signed, witnessed and dated, money changes hands and there are no other parties to complicate this arrangement.

## Tenancies for couples

Similarly, where couples (of either sex) take on a single unit, they enter a straightforward joint tenancy with their landlord. Both sign the same lease, meaning they have **joint and several liability** for the tenancy – in other words, each is liable for the other's commitments agreed in the lease. If one party doesn't pay rent, the other party is liable for the whole rent owed. Likewise for damage, whoever causes it, the pair of tenants always remain jointly responsible. However, many tenants take on a place with a spare room then decide to sublet it without consent. Expect much tougher restrictions on this from now on as three non-related individuals sharing a single unit may bring your landlord into costly licensing requirements. Rent a place that you can afford without subterfuge. Most tenants rent what they need, not spare space.

> The fun and games really begin with joint tenancies, which have *more than two parties signing the same lease.* This is **joint and several liability** at its most common and most complex. Hundreds of thousands of tenants up and down the country club together to afford accommodation. It can work excellently, but there are some real pitfalls for tenants (and landlords) who don't think these arrangements through thoroughly before they sign up.

## Joint tenancies

In a joint tenancy *every* tenant who signs the *same* lease is bound by the *same* terms, known legally as **joint and several liability**.

This is a very common scenario and, in any group of tenants even when they have been the best of pals, all being liable for each other can have significant implications. Here are the first four that I think of, there are 40 more combinations of complications I could have written here given space.

■ If one tenant decides to leave, and gives notice to the landlord/agent, technically the tenancy of you all can fold.

■ Alternatively, if one tenant leaves, and the others agree jointly with their landlord to stay on, the remaining tenants are responsible for the whole of the rent, not just the percentage they were each paying before.

■ Tenants need consent to replace one outgoing tenant with another person. Most managers will want to run credit checks and take up references at the very least. You can't invite perfect strangers to live in your landlord's building. It's a clear breach of the lease. Changing tenants should trigger new lease signing procedures because a new group of tenants will be creating a *new* joint and several liability lease. Where agencies are involved, expect a batch of new charges.

■ One tenant moving on will often require some arrangement for return of their deposit, triggering more charges for inventory checking to ensure no damages need paying for, prior to any refunds on deposits.

On and on run the ways that multiple occupation can cause headaches on both sides of the contract. Make sure if you agree to move in with others and tie yourself into this type of arrangement, that *all of you* will be able to stay the course of your initial fixed term or absolute chaos can ensue.

> Leaving home is supposed to be a liberating experience, not a legal minefield, so sort yourselves out well in advance.

### Complexities of joint tenancies

Here I'm just scratching the surface to give you an idea of how they work, but joint tenancies are complex, as are a number of other ways of occupying houses either as groups, or collections of individuals. But, like licences, many thousands of successful joint and several liability tenancies are set up, run well and conclude happily each and every year, without a hitch.

Although brilliantly successful, there are significant safety issues that the government has finally addressed in its **2004 Housing Acts** – in a valiant effort to raise standards for sharers, who are often the least financially equipped people and who some in our industry seem to unfortunately regard as 'fair game' for lousy conditions. (See Lesson 14 on Houses in Multiple Occupation for some strict new legislation to protect you. Frankly, together with deposit protection, this government has made real efforts to protect private rented tenants. Bravo!)

Joint tenancies are quite complicated to run for landlords/agents too. It can be really difficult for example when one tenant wants to leave, *and* wants their share of the deposit back. The landlord or agent won't give back any part of the deposit before the property has been vacated and inspected. In some cases they *will* let you find another sharer, and the new tenant can 'buy out' the outgoing tenant's share of the deposit by paying them direct.

> If you are the new tenant, make sure the landlord or agent has your name on the lease, or the ultimate deposit return can go to the person you've just paid off.

In these circumstances you're all likely to need a brand new lease tricky for the tenants, tricky for the landlord when tenants have already used up most of their first fixed term and don't *want* another whole six months' liability. (This could be a situation for good, trustworthy tenants to be offered a new tenancy on a **contractual periodic** basis. However it's always a difficult call for landlords/agents simply because guaranteed 'no fault' possession slips six months into the future each time a new lease is signed.)

If one party doesn't pay their share of the rent on time the rest of you will have to make it up. If one party causes major damage you are all jointly responsible for the total cost. Many a large deposit has evaporated in this way. These tenancies can be messy and fraught with unseen problems. You need to thrash out all these types of issues *before* you embark on one.

## Multiple individual tenancies in a single dwelling

If joint tenancies are tricky, sharing the same house with strangers can be infinitely trickier. If four people share a building and each has signed an individual lease, co-ordination can be a nightmare and lead to very disruptive lifestyles. Who's responsible for cleaning up? For reporting faults? How are bills shared? How can the outgoing tenant get at least a part of their deposit back? Will s/he get it back from the management – or from the incoming tenant?

Say one gives notice to quit, while the other three wish to stay on, the landlord faces either a period of three-quarters rent (because no tenant is liable for anyone's rent but their own), or the unenviable task of trying to find another single person to fit in with the existing tenants – who can deliberately make people feel pretty unwelcome if they've already formed a tight clique. Besides which, these type of leases rarely all start and finish simultaneously. The landlord then faces the impossible task of trying to assess who is responsible for what damage or mess, as one tenant demands a deposit return when they move out, and all the others deny responsibility for a thing. (Again, an interesting situation that arbitrators of the new tenancy deposit schemes may struggle with too!)

> Simply because combining a number of tenants in one property can be so complicated, agents and landlords will usually only accept sharing on a joint and several liability basis, where every tenant signs one single lease, inventory, schedules, etc. And no wonder.

### Families (parents and children)

Families will usually be regarded by management as a single group or household. Adults will sign the single lease. No one aged under 18 is legally allowed to enter a contract. While few families choose to rent for long, many find themselves renting to cover short gaps, perhaps between buying/selling houses. Other family groups may be housed by landlords on Housing Benefit arrangements as a more long-term agreement. In these circumstances that same joint and several liability principle applies to the household members.

## Oral agreements

Tenants and landlords may not have a written agreement but a verbal one. (Please check out Lesson 7 where your contract rights and responsibilities are explained a bit more.)

Some landlords prefer to not give anything in writing; presumably believing that they have given away less rights this way. This isn't the case. Not for either party. Tenants' drawbacks are immense where no paperwork framework exists. It can be almost impossible for tenants to prove that they haven't agreed to a fixed term of, say, one year, which would allow their landlord or agency to pursue them for any rent or outgoings during this period, unless they have something in writing. Both parties are much better protected with some written evidence of their contract.

Given tenants' vulnerability without written details of their tenancies, they are entitled in law to certain details in writing, if their tenancy began after 28 February 1997. Any tenant can make a written request to their landlord for the following details, and the landlord is obliged to provide, within 28 days, a written confirmation of:

- the date the tenancy began
- the amount of rent payable, and the dates on which it should be paid
- any rent review arrangements
- the length of any fixed term which has been agreed.

If your landlord refuses to provide this written statement or ignores your letter, you can get in touch with the local authority or the Citizens' Advice Bureaux, and they will help you. The landlord is actually liable to be fined if they won't provide you with this basic statement. For those of you who rent through agencies, and who have not been given the address of your landlord, write to the landlord via your agency. If the agent will not forward your written request for a statement, again contact one of the sources previously given, as you have a legal entitlement to be provided at least with the basic framework of your tenancy on paper.

### Oral tenancies which started before February 1997

Some tenants with oral tenancies, which were agreed *before* February 1997 and are still running now, may in fact have the benefit of an assured tenancy, because, as was mentioned in Lesson 7, many landlords did not realise that prior to that date, by failing to serve a Section 20 notice on their prospective tenant before the tenancy began, they were automatically creating an assured tenancy, with *much* more security. Again, what your landlord said can be much less significant than when they said it. If you think that this applies to your current circumstances, make an appointment and take advice.

## Who is responsible for repairs?

### Landlord responsibilities

With an exception that is unlikely to affect any assured shorthold tenant or licensee (i.e. leases of longer than seven years), all landlords have a statutory repairing obligation on them under the Landlord and Tenant Act 1985 for the following.

- The structure and exterior of the property, which usually includes drains, gutters and external pipes.
- Baths, basins, toilets, showers and other sanitary fittings.
- Heating and hot water facilities.
- Gas and electrical services.

They are liable under different legislation for furniture safety, gas safety and for environmental health, fire safety requirements plus liabilities under common and civil law.

### Tenant responsibilities

The tenant is under a legal obligation to behave in a tenant-like manner, and to conduct themselves in a way which will take care of the property. Routine care is implied in all tenancy agreements – this includes both the building *and* its contents.

- Turning off water or boilers, e.g. when going away in the winter if the heating is switched off. Better still, if the weather's cold, leave the heating on low and continuously to prevent problems while you're away.

- Mending fuses, replacing light bulbs, etc.

- Unblocking sinks, or other, which they have blocked with their own waste.

In addition tenants are responsible for not damaging the property, either deliberately or carelessly, and for ensuring that their guests don't either.

### Repair issues

Always know exactly where to report faults or problems to, before you move in. All faults and any accidental damage should be immediately reported to your landlord/agent. However some things require immediate action on the tenant's behalf like turning off services that have faults. Always report any action to your landlord/tenant as soon as practicable.

Before you move in ask the landlord/agent how to operate the fuse box and how to turn off all electricity should a serious incident occur. Familiarise yourself with the gas supply and make sure you know how to turn off the whole supply in the event of possible leaks.

Ask where the stopcock for the mains water supply is, in case a pipe bursts, so that you can cut off the water.

### Suspected gas leaks

All suspected gas leaks should be reported direct to Transco (number under Gas in *Yellow Pages*) who will give you advice over the phone. Also notify your landlord/agent that you've done this and ask for advice.

*Major problems*

If the problem is major (no heat, faulty cooking facilities, a broken fridge) landlords/agents should begin dealing with this immediately (say within 24 hours). If they don't, make a second call within 48 hours. If they still haven't organised essential repairs, write to them formally and complain, recorded delivery.

> Never try fixing anything that is part of the services *nor* which belongs to the landlord. You could get hurt – or even end up liable for a bill, for making things worse.

Lost keys are urgent and infuriating. Look after your keys or expect to be charged for key callouts.

Where landlords ignore repeated requests for repairs that are their obvious responsibility, take advice from one of the many services suggested earlier which help tenants with troublesome landlords.

### Where tenant responsibilities lie

Remember, you cannot hold your landlord/agent responsible for the consequences of damage if you haven't notified them that a problem exists. Nor can you hold your management responsible for damage to your own things caused by unreported problems.

For example slowly leaking pipes can wreak havoc in units. If you find evidence of water coming out of anything but a tap, there's a real problem and it needs reporting immediately. Not reporting obvious problems – especially ones with potential knock-on effects – could be construed as negligent conduct.

# Lesson 10

# When you decide to leave

Despite all the perceptions, the vast majority of tenancies end when tenants decide to leave, not when landlords insist that they go. When you decide that the time has come to move on, or your fixed term is nearing its end and you don't wish to stay on, you need to organise yourself all over again.

## Giving formal notice

Just like when beginning one, legal contracts need formal closure.

- If you're choosing to leave at the end of a fixed term, notify your landlord/agent in writing at least one calendar month in advance.

- Similarly, if you decide to move on at some later stage, it's still essential that you let your landlord/agent know – in writing, recorded delivery unless it's handed in to an agency, so there's no confusion – at least a calendar month before.

- Date the letter, and give the exact leaving date in the letter.

- Send all correspondence to shut down contracts via recorded delivery – just to avoid any confusion.

- If there are any special terms or conditions in your lease, follow them.

Furthermore, if you have been happy and well cared for, legal requirements aside, courtesy still is appreciated and can prove valuable long term. Remember, you may want to come back here for a reference, say for a future rental, or even for a mortgage application.

The leaving date you are giving is *legally binding*; you can't just change your mind if your new job falls through. If anything does happen within the formal notice period which makes you want to stay longer than your given leaving date, you need to contact the agency or landlord very quickly. If they have not already agreed a contract with someone else, they will probably be happy to work something out. Even if they have, if you have a track record of being a good tenant the 'bird in the hand' theory will probably help you to persuade them in your favour.

If they have found someone that they prefer however, perhaps at a higher rent, you are unlikely to persuade them to accommodate your needs and you will be expected to move out as legally stated in writing.

## What to do next

As soon as you give notice, check through your lease to find out what requirements have been put in for vacating the property, *and there will be some.* This is also an excellent time to remember that some agencies (and a few landlords) make significant profits from the cleaning and redecoration of properties when tenancies change hands. Some of the requirements that have been made may take a bit of time, but still need doing. This is the rubber gloves moment that I mentioned earlier. It can take a while to get things ship shape in a unit you've been living in all year – especially if you're at work most of the time and haven't cleaned the oven out as you went along.

### The 28-day clause

As mentioned earlier, when you look at your lease you are also likely to find in here a clause that allows, within reason, the landlord or agent to show prospective new tenants around the property during the notice period. Tenants who have got along well with their management may well be asked to tidy up a bit when new tenants are viewing. OK, you're not obliged to do it, but if you've had a happy time and you'd like a reference, it's not an unreasonable request.

### If you are giving notice within the fixed term

It's very much in your interests to help your landlord find a new tenant as quickly as possible by letting them do viewings with the place looking its shiny best. If tenants do give notice during their fixed term, they'll still have a rental liability until the end of that period. However, landlords/agents are still obliged to 'take reasonable steps to find a suitable replacement'. If this is happening, helping them by being co-operative is a good idea. Some of the best services I know do genuinely try reducing their tenants' potential losses, when tenants suddenly have to move out for good reason, and as I have said before there are a large number of reasonable landlords around.

## Moving out

Before you leave you must ensure that everything in the property is *exactly* as you found it. Here a well-organised inventory really comes into its own. You need to clean thoroughly. *Everywhere*. It is no good taking a nice clean house or flat, leaving it in a state and expecting no consequences. Leaving a mess behind will cost you money and cause you hassle.

■ Take every room, clean every mark off the walls, wash every inch of floor. (Yes, even behind the loo.) (I know many landlords who always rent by preference to tenants who have been in the armed forces because they are marched into and out of all their service quarters under full inspection. The Swedes have a very strict regime where specialist cleaners must be used by both parties at each end of the rental contract. Even the ball cocks are scrubbed clean under this system.)

■ You need to defrost fridges, and wash them out thoroughly. Don't unplug the fridge and close the door – mould forms immediately. Either switch off and leave the door open when you leave, or leave it switched on with the door closed.

■ Clean cookers – the bane of every landlord's life – and those grease-filled cooker hoods. It takes *hours* to pull a cooker back from a state and tenants will find their deposit disappearing fast if they don't clean up thoroughly.

■ Wash the *insides* of cupboards as well as the doors. Hoover everywhere – including under the beds.

■ The list is endless. Make the place look exactly as it did the day you moved in. Leave nothing to chance, or indeed to charge.

■ If it is a term of your lease and you signed it, you need to take drapes to the dry cleaners and provide a receipt. If linen has been provided, wash and iron it and leave it where you found it.

These are just the standard terms. Your own lease can have other requirements, and you need to observe them or you may well end up with other pre-agreed charges.

Tenants in expensive units are advised to employ a professional cleaning service and save the receipt. Less room for claim and counter-claim this way.

And finally, replace anything you have broken or damaged to the same standard. Having cleaned thoroughly, replaced light-bulbs, etc, check around to make sure the furniture is in the same rooms as when you moved in. I know landlords who will shove an armchair back into the lounge, but agencies will call out the maintenance man. You have been warned.

## *You're joking, right?*

No I am not. Landlords and agents get sick and tired of being expected to clean up after other people for free. It means the unit cannot go straight back on the market until someone has pulled it back up to scratch. Remember that the balance of responsibility is yours, not your landlord's or agent's. While many are just delighted to get back a lovely clean property and happy to return your deposit in exchange, sadly others are waiting for the tiniest detail for a deposit reduction.

When you are satisfied, repeat the photo process I suggested in the Lesson on inventories or call in someone else you can trust (not your mum) to verify the clean standard of return. This can seem like an awful palaver, but many of you will have lost money over this process in the past, and almost all of you will know someone else who has. Again, fingers crossed that the new Tenancy Deposit Scheme begins chipping away at the routine charges many agents and landlords try for.

### *Final accounts*

- Don't forget to notify gas, telephone and electricity companies of exactly when you are leaving, and, as you move out, *take a meter reading* to check against your closing accounts.

- Tell the local authority and water companies that you are leaving too.

- Give everyone a forwarding address for the sending of final accounts.

- Those of you wanting to speed up deposit returns may well consider settling final bills over the phone with a debit card and asking for a verifiable payment number. Others will visit council offices, pay their final accounts and get receipts for doing so.

All these things help landlords/agents make the speediest deposit refunds. If you've been one of the many silly tenants who believed that by keeping a low profile you'd get away with costs, think again. Landlords/agents automatically provide all the authorities and utilities with details of new tenants – in the end, your liabilities will always catch up with you.

> Provide everyone with a forwarding address (these are an important part of the process for many deposit returns) and return *all* keys wherever requested. If keys aren't returned, you may well end up being billed to have the locks changed.

## Once you have left

Having left the property and given back the keys you may find that some private landlords inspect that day, and send your deposit to your provided forwarding address immediately. A few may even inspect just before you leave and pay you there and then, but this is *rare*. Most landlords/agents need a bit of time in an empty unit to go through the place with their own inventory and few of us appreciate having the tenant present, breathing down our necks in what must be a detailed process. It's also likely to become even rarer with the new deposit systems.

Most agencies and private landlords, quite reasonably, not only check the building, but need formal confirmation that you have settled all your final accounts before moving on. Given the number of tenants who try to leave behind a mountain of debts, this is a sensible precaution for managers to take. As well as the work involved, no new tenant wants to move into any property which has unpaid bills outstanding, or bad payment records. Each new tenant is entitled to a 'clean sheet'. Properties with records of County Court judgments can be a nightmare to move in to, as no one will give the new tenants any credit without immense amounts of hassle.

If you haven't paid your own bills, don't be surprised if your deposit is used to pay them. New systems are being brought in to protect tenants from abuse, not to allow them to avoid settling their own debts.

### The dreaded time lag

The new rules will insist that deposit refunds reach tenants within ten days. Unfortunately, the length of time that (even within reasonable practices) it takes to receive your original deposit back from one property, in order to make a move, can leave people trapped. If you are utterly dependent on the deposit held by one landlord to pay the deposit on the next unit, and you want to move from one to the other immediately (as most of us do), you can have real difficulty. The value of having a good relationship with your existing landlord is again obvious.

However it's not always possible to get a landlord/agent to co-operate, and some landlords can be very oppressive about this. There are unfortunately no easy solutions to needing your deposit back from an unco-operative landlord or agent, to enable you to move to something better. It really is a Catch 22 situation, which no amount of experience can really resolve, and one which bad practitioners can, and regrettably *do* exploit, leaving poorer tenants vulnerable and understandably frustrated. I'm not even certain how the new system can help those who need their deposit back to move on within 24 hours. Not everyone has a helpful bank manager, or a generous parent to tide us over a critical ten days. Let's hope for better things after April 2007, where at least an obligation for part/full refunds becomes ten days.

For those of you using independent landlords, with whom you've enjoyed a good business relationship, there's at least a chance of fast movement.

> Do your best to co-operate by handing back a clean, debt-free unit and you may well be surprised at how co-operative your landlord can be in return.

## Deposits taken from tenants at any time before 6 April 2007

There are two letters in Appendix 4 that you could find helpful if you are experiencing any difficulty in obtaining a deposit refund (under the old system, which will still affect tenants for quite some time yet). The first is a polite letter to be copied out and posted ten days after you vacate, if you are still waiting. Enclose photocopies of any receipts etc. The second is a much stronger letter to be posted within seven days of the first, if you are still waiting. Once it ever becomes necessary to start writing for your deposit, you have reached the stage when you *must* register all letters so that you can prove that you have written.

## If your money still doesn't arrive

Tenants who have returned the property they have been renting in good condition, and have proof that no outstanding bills remain unsettled, should have absolutely no hesitation in both threatening and then taking action for its recovery in the Small Claims Court (see letter in Appendix 4). These are inexpensive and effective. In most cases simply sounding well informed, and writing a letter that sounds competent, will be sufficient to concentrate the mind of whoever it is who is being slow. Your Citizens' Advice Bureau will write letters on your behalf, as will local law centres. If you have also made your own accurate provisions for proof (photos and witnesses), as suggested earlier, you will be even better protected.

# Lesson 11

# When your landlord tells you to leave or seeks legal possession

There is a world of difference between mutual agreement to leave units and the formal use of **possession proceedings**. There is also a limit to what I can explain here because the range of circumstances is vast. However, always understand that all assured shorthold tenancies have available, by their very design, a 'no fault' basis for landlords to claim back their property via the courts, so long as they comply with certain rules and so long as either your initial fixed term has expired or a minimum of six months has elapsed from the start of the tenancy.

> This guide is intended for general information only about the broad framework of how things fit together, not as a substitute for legal advice that covers your specific situation. Tenants being asked to leave must always seek immediate advice from one of the many sources given earlier.

There are a few common reasons why things don't work out to create a long term, enduring tenancy.

- If a landlord/agent seeks a rent increase at the end of a fixed term that you can't or won't agree to.

- If the landlord/agent told you at the beginning of your tenancy that they would definitely want the building back at the end of a fixed term. (This often happens when people rent out their own homes for short periods then need to move back home.)

- However, *the main reason* that landlords tell tenants to leave is that they are not happy with the way the tenancy has been progressing. In other words, the obvious way to avoid being asked to leave is simply to keep your side of the bargain.

# When this can happen

Where serious breaches of tenancies arise, landlords/agents have a perfect right to ask courts to terminate tenancies. This can happen at any time – for *serious* breaches. In circumstances that are serious, landlords will simply use another element of the law, other than their 'no fault' rights – often referred to as a **Section 8**. Court forms will duly arrive through your letterbox. Gone are the days when tenants could pretty much cause mayhem, tenant behaviour is expected to be reasonable – at all times. I have included a list of the legal reasons (known as Grounds) that your landlord/agent may apply to court for at the end of this Lesson. I have also included the timescales that the courts can use if you are making a significant nuisance of yourself.

Your protections under the assured shorthold legislation are limited to the fixed term and even the fixed term doesn't allow you to breach the lease, say by not paying rent or causing damage. Beyond that fixed term (or six months for periodic tenancies), with *no* breaches at all, your landlord enjoys the legal 'no fault' right to possession – and courts will grant them that, so long as they applied using the correct procedures.

> There is no legal case you can present once either the fixed term has expired or, with a periodic tenancy, six months has elapsed. It's the whole basis of the legislation.

### How long a written notice period must my landlord/agent give me?

It depends entirely on the circumstances – please check out the end of Lesson list. There you will see that some tenancy breaches are so serious that landlords/agents can ask for possession fairly quickly and on very short notice.

However the main reason that landlords use assured shortholds is simply that, if they give two months' written notice and cite their Section 21 rights, courts will give them possession without a hitch. This is the reason why most tenancies limp through their first few months. Using other Grounds for possession can cost more financially and has no guarantee of success. Landlords/agents who are experiencing problems with tenants from an early stage are likely to serve notice formally four months into the fixed term, meaning that they can apply to court immediately the fixed term/six months protection has ended if they're using their guaranteed rights.

### If all this sounds a bit harsh

You have to bear in mind the scale of the investment that your landlord has had to make. Though the overwhelming majority of tenants try to get things right, a significant minority reap chaos and havoc. You've smiled at the anecdotes about the washing machine, the puppy, the landlord's entire stock of furniture being sold, been shocked by the tale of the coffee grounds and cigarette ends – but I'm afraid these are landlord realities. Well here's another – I could fill a whole book with nothing but anecdotes. Unfortunately they're too common not to have some safeguards against.

### WARNING ANECDOTE

A private landlord was concerned about the volume of foot traffic going into and out of their downstairs flat. Mentioning it to the tenant seemed to have no impact. Other tenants in the block began complaining. Discussion seemed to centre around a possibility of drug dealing. The landlord sent the tenant a notice that they intended visiting 24 hours later. Arriving as planned, they found the locks had been changed. This is the time that any landlord realises the need to act. Notice to quit was duly served and, as so often happens in these cases, the tenants disappeared in the middle of the night.

However, on entering the landlord discovered their freshly decorated flat had been updated. The ceilings were painted pitch black – metal 'glow in the dark' stars had been nailed into place. The walls were painted luminous purple and a huge hoarding sign (designed for a billboard) of horses charging dominated the entire room and (predictably) had been stuck down with a permanent glue.

Just imagine for a moment how you'd feel, faced with behaviour like this. Bills to rectify damage on this scale run into many thousands of pound and weeks of lost rent sorting them out. That's why landlords have safeguards!

## Home truths

If your fixed term is coming towards a close, so long as you are being given the statutory two months' written notification, you will not get a different decision from the court however long you wish to pursue the matter. The landlord/agent is legally entitled to require possession and is exercising their automatic and guaranteed right (under something called a Section 21 of the Housing Act 1988, which will be mentioned in the written notice).

If you *had* a fixed term tenancy and this ended some time ago, the landlord can exercise this right at any time (again with two months' notice). The six months protection you enjoyed started at the beginning of your original tenancy. S/he can also apply later than the fixed term on a wider range of other grounds – some of which get him/her possession faster.

### If you are still in your fixed term

The landlord/agent can only apply to the court for a possession order on quite limited grounds until it ends. S/he cannot exercise their **guaranteed right** until the fixed term ends. But s/he can still successfully use other legal grounds *if you're breaking the terms you agreed to keep*. To do this, landlords/agents use specific legal procedures provided by the 1988 Housing Act and strengthened in 1996 to protect landlords from tenants who deliberately misuse their property.

However applications to courts are not frivolous things. Landlords/agents tend only to act if tenants have given them some really good reason to do so. For those tenants with a fixed term that has still not expired, your landlord can only apply to the court for possession on Grounds 2, 8, 10, 15 and 17, and only if the tenancy agreement made provision for it.

> I cannot emphasise strongly enough, *real security of tenure* almost always rests in a tenant's own hands. Good tenancies don't get closed down on a whim.

### *If you have a contractual periodic tenancy*

Your landlord can apply to the court at any time from the start of the tenancy on a wider range of grounds. But again, these legal grounds are significant breaches of the lease – all in your own hands. If s/he is exercising their Section 21 right, where s/he's guaranteed possession that 'right' still cannot be exercised until six months have elapsed since the beginning of the tenancy. Again, you are entitled to two months' written notice for the *guaranteed* right, but not for some of the major breaches of contract. When tenancies have been problematic, expect this two months' notice to drop through the letterbox after four months.

### *Is two months' written notice always required?*

No. Other applications for possession due to breaches of lease can be much shorter, from as little as two weeks. A full list together with the timescales involved is available at the end of this Lesson.

Some tenancies break down completely, and very acrimoniously. This is almost without exception because one party or another is behaving badly. It may be the last thing that someone wants to hear, but when things have reached this stage, it really often is the best thing to move on. Use the notice period to find somewhere else to live.

On the other hand, sometimes, perfectly friendly tenancies are concluded because the fixed term has expired, and no agreement on a new rent can be reached.

---

**WARNING ANECDOTE**

One hard working agent had a problem on their hands. The tenant had lost their job and had made all the arrangements for Housing Benefit – including signing over the future payments direct to the agent. However Housing Benefit is notoriously lackadaisical – a ten to 12 week delay is common – the agent understood this and knew that a cheque for all back payments would eventually arrive. However the landlord was not so understanding. Shouting and yelling in the agency, he withdrew his business and his keys from the agent and departed to throw the unwary tenant out on his ear. All the horrified agent could do was telephone the tenant and warn them to call the police.

Tenants told to leave without written notice, or worse just ordered out, should seek *immediate* advice from their local housing department, law centre or CAB – or call out the police. Your landlord simply cannot order you out, nor pack your things and move them out. All tenants still enjoy the legal right to stay in place until the *court* has both granted a possession order and the court has then enforced it – never the landlord direct. It remains the exclusive right of the court both to grant and enforce possession orders. At the bottom end of the market, some deeply disturbing things happen to tenants. These are covered in Lesson 13, Harassment and Illegal Eviction.

## What to do next

Don't assume however that because you have to leave that you need necessarily have further problems. Tenants who have been given notice can, if they have caused no damage, left no debts, and left the property in the same condition as they accepted it, fully expect and are still legally entitled to their deposit refund once all legitimate liabilities have been settled. Follow the advice in the previous lessons, and claim your refund.

### Cutting your losses

Deposit refunds will obviously be more difficult if the landlord wants possession because you have damaged their property or owe small fortunes in rent. Tenants who have lost their home because they have behaved badly should seriously consider cutting their losses. Landlords/agents with a valid possession order are not about to take your conduct lying down. If you owe rent or have caused damage beyond the limit of your deposit, landlords/agents are able to additionally sue you in the county court for all outstanding debts plus owed rent – and they are likely to get a favourable response. You could end up with the distinction of having lost your home, all your deposit, plus having to pay extra to your landlord *and* having a County Court judgement recorded against you. Hardly ideal, and rather difficult to find somewhere else to live, given the common use of tenant blacklists and credit rating services.

However, in all cases, whatever the grounds for possession and however long or short the notice period must be, the landlord/agent is always obliged to give the tenant a form of written notice.

> No tenant can find that they have lost their home without any prior knowledge.

Beyond the notice – I emphasise again – landlords/agents must use courts for possession and court bailiffs for evictions. *No* landlord can act directly – not under any circumstances whatsoever.

## Possession orders

There are two basic types of possession order.

- **Absolute possession orders**, where the court orders possession on one of the Mandatory Grounds or when the landlord is exercising their shorthold rights to possession using Section 21. These are non negotiable directives to quit the property by a certain date.

- **Suspended possession orders**, where a Discretionary Ground has been used, and the court *may* decide to allow the tenant to stay on, so long as they meet certain conditions set down by the court. If these conditions are breached, clearly your landlord/agent can go straight back to court.

> This system is complex. Any tenant caught up in these situations should seek immediate legal advice to guide them through the process in detail.

Once a possession order has been granted, it will specify the exact date that a tenant must leave by. If the tenant doesn't go, the landlord simply goes back to court, pays a small fee and court appointed bailiffs will arrive to evict you.

### A harsh, rarely recognised reality

One of the sadder reasons that tenants end up behind with their rent is when they lose their jobs. If this happens to you, get straight onto your landlord/agent and explain. Many (especially those who regularly deal with cheaper units) will understand the time lag between genuine Housing Benefit applications and your benefit actually arriving. Most will ask you to ensure that cheques reach them direct, rather than via your own hands and that seems a reasonable tradeoff for their considerable patience. As an industry we've been complaining for years about these ridiculously long periods of time for Housing Benefit arrival – but no one listens!

Some landlords/agents will ask you to leave because they have a policy of not accepting unemployed tenants full stop. Others will bide their time. Some will say yes, then hassle you, week on week making your life even more difficult. If this happens, ask for paperwork from the Housing Benefit team to reassure your landlord that things are crawling along – otherwise they may get agitated and start serving notices to quit.

However, some people don't always get great choices in life. Few young people would get much more than hysterical laughter if they asked for council/housing association accommodation and so they, in particular, are *forced* into the private rental sector – a purely commercial service that exists exclusively to make a profit. You may find an understanding landlord, but we are certainly not social workers. Plus, modern rentals are relatively expensive for people on low wages.

> A bitter reality is that tenants finding themselves in deep financial trouble *will always be advised to stay put* by every advising body and legal body – *even when a dated possession order has already been granted.* What many of the general public (including many landlords/agents) often don't realise is that – by moving out without an actual eviction (i.e. the bailiffs actually arriving) – tenants are classified by local authorities as having made themselves *voluntarily* homeless.

That means that they get no housing help/temporary shelter. In other words, sometimes the only way that a tenant in trouble can get *any* choice but sleeping in the rain is to remain until the bitter end – infuriating landlords and agents who don't understand the complexity of local authority processes. It's bureaucracy at its absolute worst – but it's today's maddening reality.

### Accelerated possession procedures

These may be used by landlords to speed up the legal process, but only if the tenant has a written tenancy agreement and your fixed term has expired (including when your tenancy has continued on to become a statutory periodic). Your landlord must give you the appropriate written notice and follow correct procedure. There are special rules that apply to this fast track possession process, and tenants in receipt of notice of accelerated possession proceedings should seek pretty prompt legal advice.

### Grounds for possession

A Ground is a legal reason. A *Mandatory Ground* is one where the court *must* grant a possession order to the landlord. A *Discretionary Ground* is one where the court *may* grant a possession order to the landlord. Some of these grounds require prior notice to have been served on the tenant before the tenancy was agreed, in order to forewarn tenants that the landlord might apply to the court. Seek legal advice wherever you are unsure of your position.

## Summary of Grounds for seeking possession

### Mandatory Grounds

### Ground 1
That the landlord gave the tenant written notice at the start of the tenancy that they used to live in the property as their only, or main home. (Or, in certain circumstances, that they or their wife require it to live in as their main home.)

### Ground 2
That the landlord has served a prior notice on the tenant at the beginning of the tenancy stating that they used to live the property as their only or main home, and the property was subject to a mortgage granted before the tenancy started and that the lender wants to sell it, usually to pay off mortgage arrears.

### Ground 3
That the tenancy is for a fixed term not exceeding eight months, and at some time during the 12 months before the tenancy started, the property was let or licensed for a holiday.

### Ground 4
A notice was served on the tenant at the start of the tenancy and the

tenancy is a fixed term tenancy not exceeding 12 months, that at some time during the 12 months before the tenancy began the property was let by a specified educational establishment to students.

### Ground 5
A notice was served on the tenant at the beginning of the tenancy stating that the property is held for use by a minister of religion, and is now required for that purpose.

### Ground 6
The landlord intends to demolish or redevelop the property and cannot do so with the tenant living there. This Ground cannot be used where the landlord can do the work around the tenant without them having to move, nor can it be used where the landlord or someone before them bought the property with an existing tenant, usually a sitting tenant. The tenant's removal expenses have to be met.

### Ground 7
The former tenant, who must have had either a contractual or statutory periodic, has died in the previous 12 months and no one living at the property has a right to succeed to the tenancy.

### Ground 8
The tenant owes at least two months' rent, or eight weeks if the rent is weekly based, at the time the landlord served notice and this amount is still outstanding at the date of the court hearing.

## Discretionary Grounds

### Ground 9
Suitable alternative accommodation is available for the tenant or will be from the date the order takes effect (the Housing Act 1988 defines suitable alternative accommodation). The tenant's removal costs will be met.

### Ground 10
The tenant was behind with the rent, both when notice of seeking possession was served and when court proceedings began.

## Ground 11
Although the tenant was not behind with the rent when the landlord started possession proceedings, they have been persistently late with their rent.

## Ground 12
The tenant has broken one or more of the terms of their tenancy agreements, except the obligation to pay rent.

## Ground 13
The condition of the property has become worse because of the behaviour of the tenant, their sub-tenant, or any other person living there.

## Ground 14
The tenant, or someone living with the tenant, or visiting the tenant, has caused, or is likely to cause, a nuisance or annoyance to other persons living in, or visiting the locality; or that any of them have been convicted of using the property or allowing it to be used for immoral or illegal purposes, or have committed an arrestable offence in or in the locality of the property.

## Ground 15
The condition of the furniture has become worse, because it has been ill-treated by the tenant, their sub-tenant, or someone else living in the property.

## Ground 16
The tenancy was granted because the tenant was employed by the landlord, or a former landlord, and the tenant is no longer employed by the landlord.

## Ground 17
The landlord was persuaded to grant the tenancy on the basis of a false statement made knowingly or recklessly by the tenant or any person acting at the tenant's instigation.

Where any of these Grounds are applied to you, seek immediate legal advice on receipt.

## Notice periods for each Ground

■ For Grounds: 3, 4, 8, 10, 11, 12, 13, 15 and 17, at least two weeks' written notice is required.

■ For Grounds: 1, 2, 5, 6, 7, 9 and 16, at least two months' written notice is required.

■ Ground 14 has been strengthened by the 28 February 1997 revisions. Landlords may start proceedings as soon as they have served written notice.

All notices should state in writing the full Grounds that the landlord is intending to base their application upon. All these official documents will reach you via a court. There is no specific Ground for guaranteed possession rights of landlords. All landlords/agents need to do is write to you citing their Section 21 rights and wait long enough to comply with the court's paperwork.

# Lesson 12

# How your landlord's mortgage can affect you

During the 1980s some press coverage about this issue started to filter out. The lettings business was booming because no one could sell their house, and negative equity (where your house is worth less than you borrowed to pay for it) hit hundreds of thousands of homeowners. Although the issue has gone off the media boil now, the buy to let phenomenon means that landlord borrowing is now through the roof. The fact that your landlord might well have borrowed large sums of money to buy the house you're living in can have some interesting effects on you.

## Looking for trouble

Expect a return to these awkward times if the current boom ends. It still haunts the industry – not all rental units prove viable in lean times – meaning what the landlord can get in rent doesn't cover their costs and that's when the trouble starts. It's an awful situation to find yourself in. You've dutifully paid the rent, but the landlord has spent it rather than paying their lender, and lenders can move with surprising speed to get *vacant* possession (meaning tenants must go). Again, due legal process is always required.

Most rented property is now bought with borrowed money. Special deals for investment in rented property have emerged and new landlords are entering the housing supply market. This is absolutely great, and is where most new rentals have come from.

> However, even if you dutifully pay your rent, some landlords don't dutifully pay their mortgages. A debt can still be building up against the property, with legal consequences which can literally mean you losing your home, despite it not being your fault in any way.

Of course, this doesn't happen too often, but if it affects you, the fact that you are in a minority doesn't make you feel one jot better. To a certain extent this is a risk you take, however being completely unaware that it exists doesn't seem completely sensible.

Actually almost all normal mortgages have a clause in them, which prohibits the borrower subletting without authority from the lender (bank, building society). For the majority of tenants this causes absolutely no problem, as the owner uses the rent to pay the mortgage and no one is any the wiser. These days landlords gaily borrow money in the expectation of making huge gains, while tenants pay the monthly costs. But life has a funny way of not running to plan – especially where landlords overreach themselves, as can so often happen when prices are skyrocketing.

Life soon changes for tenants when the landlord is in personal financial difficulty and doesn't keep making their monthly payments. As the number of repossessions (where the lender goes to court for a possession order) is again slowly creeping back up again, tenants can sometimes experience real problems that they are powerless to control.

In theory, anyone who has borrowings against a property they are letting out should serve a special notice, called **Prior Notice**, on their tenants advising them that the lender may want to sell it (usually to cover landlord default on mortgage payments), but in practice many don't bother. Sometimes landlords are not being deliberately misleading. You actually have to know quite a bit about the lettings industry even to be aware of this rule, unless your lender insists on it. Like all lettings rules, it gets broken mainly because it's nigh on impossible to enforce.

### What you can do

Any tenant can find out if their landlord has a mortgage. If you want to find out, you can fill out a special form online from the HM Land Registry. Currently the charge is only £4 and the Land Registry are helpfully turning these around in about 48 hours. While it won't tell you if your landlord is in financial difficulty, the name of the lender may well be on this document. At least with the name of the lender in your file, you have a chance of trying to sort this out if you become aware of problems. Start worrying when endless official looking mail addressed to your landlord regularly ends up falling through your door. If you use an agent, make sure that all this mail is promptly delivered to them – many agents don't know what's going on until it's much too late either.

Unfortunately, often the first thing a tenant knows is that a possession order has been issued through the courts from the lender. Most tenants do find out at least at this stage, because there is often an agreement that the possession order be addressed to the landlord and all occupants, which does mean you are able to open it, even if you don't like what you read.

Where this doesn't happen, the court will usually try to make sure something similar does, as they are aware that tenants often live in properties that the landlord has claimed to live in as their own home, which are suddenly subject to possession orders in favour of the lender.

The alternative would be that the court process would be completed and the bailiffs possibly arrive before an unsuspecting tenant even realised what was happening.

## Act quickly

If you're ever unlucky enough to find yourself in these circumstances you must act very quickly. If a possession order does come through your door it will have the date that the possession becomes effective already on it. If you have been aware for some time that financial difficulties surround your landlord (e.g. loads of mail and no forwarding address), apply through the county court on a form N224 to be **joined to the proceedings**. This means that although you still won't be able to stop the possession, you may be given a little extra time in which to find somewhere else to live before the locks are changed.

In any of these circumstances don't just sit around worrying or hoping the situation will somehow disappear. It is already deeply serious once lenders begin taking action. Make an immediate appointment with your local Citizens' Advice Bureau, Legal Aid centre, or local council. Here staff have the experience which you need to help you retrieve the best from what are truly awful circumstances. They may help you with legal paperwork, or even ask the landlord's lender at least to give you time to find new accommodation.

Tenants in this dreadful position lose out in every aspect. Deposits have been paid, and rent duly delivered, and in truth all may be lost. Theoretically you can take legal action against your landlord, because he owes you money, and you may even be entitled to compensation. However it can be very difficult indeed, especially if you don't have your landlord's current address. Let alone if you're one in a long line of creditors. Discuss all these matters with whomever you have approached for guidance.

# Lesson 13

# Harassment and illegal eviction

## Harassment

While it seems extraordinary to most of us (even those who don't exactly like our landlords and agents much), there is still a considerable distinction between practitioners who aren't very reasonable and the landlords whose conduct will be considered here.

For some tenants it can be such a huge problem that the guide would not be complete without its inclusion. While it may not affect a very high proportion of tenants, its effects can be utterly devastating, and some of the tenants affected have the types of tenancies which this guide has been designed to examine. As I mentioned elsewhere, there still exist a minority of landlords who feel above the law and who are often, so sadly, proved right by what happens as opposed to what ought to happen.

There is legislation in place: the Protection from Eviction Act, 1977. Further protection also exists for tenants under the 1988 Housing Acts. Although the offences are criminal, it isn't the police usually, but the local authority who will prosecute these crimes. If a landlord is found guilty they can receive a heavy fine and/or a prison sentence.

Harassment can take many forms. Although it can be because your landlord has a dispute with you, or is racist, or doesn't like your private life, the main cause of harassment is of course money. It most often seems to happen to people who get behind with their rent, or if the landlord could make more money from the building if the current tenant left.

### Landlords behaving badly

Whatever the motivation, its effects are often appalling. Here are a few to consider.

- Landlord's workmen doing work to the property over a very long time and in a way to maximise inconvenience.

- Landlords or their staff barging in and out of the property uninvited and repeatedly.

- Having the landlord's friend or relative move into the next flat and play loud music constantly.

- Shouting and swearing abuse at tenants.

- Changing the locks so tenants can't get into their home.

- Turning off the water, gas or electricity.

- Stealing your mail.

- Taking your possessions from your home.

- Sexual or racial abuse.

---

**WARNING ANECDOTE**

While working as a volunteer in a south London centre for the elderly, I was called out to an emergency. A lady in her late seventies lived in the top flat of a rundown four-storey house. I had a key, and went straight up. Her flat was devastated. Large slabs of heavy old lath and plaster ceiling were everywhere, some almost a metre across. The landlord had taken off the roof slates months earlier to 'encourage' her to move. If she hadn't actually been in the loo at the time the ceiling finally collapsed, she would have been dreadfully hurt. This woman had never owed a penny to anyone in her life, she was just trying to live in peace. The landlord had bought an investment property in an area of rapid gentrification. She was just in the wrong place at the wrong time.

---

Ah, but things have changed...mmmm. This happened to me less than a year ago.

---

**WARNING ANECDOTE**

Sometimes a rental property needs trading on. So last year I put a block of eight flats up for sale. The estate agent dutifully advised all tenants when viewings would occur and complied with all that was required to protect existing tenants. Knowing that their current landlord was selling up, many tenants asked me for references and referrals to new properties. By the time contracts were exchanged, only one long-term tenant remained. Given that his direct debit had dropped into our business account for more than a decade, I wrote him a glowing reference, gave the company his details and vice versa, plus a copy of his lease was sent to the new owner's solicitors. I assumed that was the end of the matter.

Within 24 hours, the tenant made his first ever telephone call with a worry. Within hours of owning the building, the new company had simply disconnected both mains water and electricity. They were currently on site with heavy building equipment and heavy-set men who angrily refused to turn his supplies back on. Feeling very threatened, my almost 60-year-old health authority adminis-trator telephoned the police – only to be advised that this was a 'civil matter' and not something they could send a policeman round to discuss with the contractors.

Yes, he had theoretical legal rights.

Yes he was entitled to due process.

Yes, he might even have won had he sued – eventually.

What actually happened owed more to good luck than good law. I advised my former tenant not to confront the gang of builders, but to prepare to leave. Within 12 hours a cousin had provided him with new accommodation and had even helped out with men and a van for a sharp exit.

What if I hadn't known someone with a vacant unit? Someone who'd take my word on a deposit transfer? Someone who'd accept a verbal reference instead of the usual credit checks and process? Let alone someone with a van and heavy-set men of his own to 'negotiate' this situation? What happens to someone when the police just won't intervene in a civil case like this – even when the tenant rightly felt physically harassed and effectively evicted by default?

With that particular experience under my belt, I shudder to think just how often this happens up and down the country when buildings change hands. I had put in place every single legal safeguard for this tenant, and the law proved completely and utterly ineffectual.

Of course, as the number of more secure tenancies has declined, some of these stories have reduced, but as you see, some tenants still end up in the hands of despotic landlords. Even with automatic rights of possession some landlords can behave appallingly if, say, tenants fall behind with their rent. If your landlord is behaving in any way that makes you uncomfortable (as opposed to irritated), get in touch with the tenancy relations officer at your local council − they are usually prompt and effective. There are laws to protect you − but, as the last anecdote shows only too clearly, unless physical violence is involved, they're not always as effective as they ought to be.

## Illegal eviction

This is usually easier for a tenant to substantiate than harassment because it is clearer. It is an eviction, which is simply not lawful, and for most tenants that means eviction by the landlord or their employees. No landlord or their agents can legally carry out evictions, this is always the preserve of the courts and their servants (bailiffs).

This is the 'suitcases in the garden' syndrome I mentioned in the Introduction. You can actually be evicted illegally from just a part of your accommodation. For example if the landlord locks off rooms in a house you are renting to deprive you of their use, a not-uncommon trick I'm afraid: 'you owe me some rent, I'm taking some space back till you've paid up.'

Even if the landlord has an absolute possession order (see Grounds for Possession) they cannot simply walk in and turf you out. If they have an order, and you haven't moved out by the date on the order, the landlord cannot personally evict tenants. S/he must use court procedures every single time − no matter how frustrated s/he's become.

In this depressing section there is one more thing I need to mention, although I hope it affects none of my readers. Although the action for both the above is taken by the local authority, if your landlord, or anyone working for them ever threatens violence, or is violent, you must contact the police, not the local authority. Sometimes they can be a little reluctant to get involved, but if you do feel under any sort of physical threat, only the police may act.

These instances may be rare — but they're not rare enough to not bother us all. As I've mentioned before, there is a rump of landlords who act in all ways as if the law of the land didn't apply to them. Heavy fines and even imprisonment await landlords who harass or illegally evict any tenant. Did any of these complex laws bother the 'landlords' who purchased the block with my former tenant in place?

No. The law of the land didn't bother to even get involved and the tenant was left high and dry.

# Lesson 14

# Houses in multiple occupation

Again, as with deposits, I am writing to try explaining legislation that hasn't bedded in yet. Under the 2004 Housing Acts the government took what many in the industry regard as swingeing steps to protect some categories of tenants who share. Legislation began on 6 April 2006 – indeed, that date is a truly momentous one for tenants. Some landlords with inadequate practice are still shaking their heads in shock at the sheer scale of the changes. 6 April 2006 marks the start date for the single biggest move towards protecting tenants that the UK has ever seen.

---

**WARNING ANECDOTE**

Local to me is a landlord/letting agent combination who is also a local magistrate. During heated exchanges about what safety rights and facilities private tenants should expect he rose to his feet.

'Why, when aeroplanes only needed one toilet per 50 passengers, was the government suggesting that he pay for one toilet between every five tenants?'

---

So let me tell you exactly what I'd have said had I been present (this incident was reported to me by a shocked MP). Tenants buy the right *to be safe* in with their rent. I'd also have made sure that this particular character knew that tenants living in bedsits (his favoured option) are *six times* likelier to die than those living in single occupancy houses. That tenants are *15 times* likelier to die if those bedsits are in buildings over three or more storeys. That something has to be done. And that, unless he fancies rent levels equivalent to the ones in the early 1970s, he shouldn't expect his tenants to live in real versions of *Life on Mars*.

## The reason for the rule changes

Since the 1980s local authorities already had legislation on their books to allow them to insist on stringent safety requirements for many old buildings/conversions and buildings over several floors. This also applied to homes with multiple 'households' – but the wording of what a 'household' comprised simply wasn't clear.

However, in the mid-1990s, a landmark legal case was fought between parties called Barnes versus Sheffield City Council. Barnes claimed that the four students sharing a house he owned all knew one another – had all signed a single joint and several liability lease – and that therefore they could be classed as one 'household'. And Barnes won.

Meaning that, no matter how squalid the conditions, where several tenants had their name on a single lease, Environmental Health Officers had to presume that the law wouldn't back them up if they tried to insist on basic, *essential* safety.

Up and down the country, this ruling was subsequently tested to virtual destruction. Students and even virtual strangers who could all be persuaded to sign a single lease could be classified as a single household – and no safety regulations could reliably be enforced unless the building fell into particular categories which certainly didn't include the standard house with several bedrooms. Safety was set back years – while rents and property prices continued to climb.

### WARNING ANECDOTE

Environmental Health Officers nationwide (EHOs are every tenant's knight in shining armour, safety wise) watched in despair, as a landlord with a huge house in Islington sought to stretch this judgment to breaking point. Despite running a rooming house, where no one in the building knew anyone else, all had separate locks on their doors, etc, this landlord tried to claim that – *simply because there was a cleaning rota for the hallway*, these tenants should also be regarded as a single household! On this occasion the landlord lost, but by now everyone concerned about tenant safety knew that new rules would have to be introduced.

The 2004 Housing Act is the result – and it has some complex implications that most tenants will never need to worry about. They cover so many issues that no one has even begun to compile a comprehensive list and I don't intend to be the first writer to try either. Very roughly speaking, expect regulations on anything hazardous that might injure tenants. And, if you rent in groups (i.e. more than two singletons together on a lease) some of this legislation may affect you.

Here's what the www.communities.gov.uk link explains (in brief). The new definition of a household gets rid of the device used in the Barnes v Sheffield case and replaces it with a sweeping definition where **a single person counts as one household and couples count as one household**.

This legislation overrides the decision to say that four students = one household. Under this legislation four students (or any other four singletons) = four households. A couple (either sex) are classified as one household – if they take in a lodger that becomes two households, i.e. couple + one = two households.

### *When does all this licensing begin?*

From 6 April 2006 if you rent property in any of the categories listed below it has become an HMO (House in Multiple Occupation) and will often (but not always) need a specific licence to operate legally. Some of these categories, those with five or more tenants or those over three or more floors, will definitely need licensing. Other types will be open to local interpretation up and down the country, local authorities decide which properties in their area need safety upgrades.

- A building which has been converted into bedsits or other non self-contained arrangements (shared bathrooms/kitchens), and where the building is let to three or more tenants) is a HMO.

- An entire house/flat where you share facilities which is let to more than two households is a HMO.

- A building converted entirely into self-contained flats before 1991, if more than a third of the flats are rented on short-term tenancies (like assured shortholds), is a HMO.

■ A converted house which contains one or more units which are not entirely self contained (i.e. ones where bathrooms/kitchens are communal), and where it contains more than two households is a HMO.

As you can see at a glance this brings an awful lot of properties under the safety umbrella of Environmental Health and some stringent safety.

## Will my landlord need a licence?

1. If the property is let to five or more individuals (including those signing a single lease and of course students) yes, your landlord will need a mandatory licence after April 2006.

2. If the property is arranged over several floors, yes they will also definitely need a mandatory license.

### Other situations

Besides those cases, many other landlords will now need to comply with tough safety rules and pay for a licence to operate certain properties as rentals. It will all depend on how each local authority decides to protect its tenants. Some (particularly those with a history of overcrowded, inadequate housing) are likely to move at speed. Others, where local conditions mean that less overcrowding exists, may not exercise all these powers . . . yet.

This legislation is far more flexible and hence far more complex than anything we've had before. Where local authorities are concerned about safety, anti-social behaviour and the adequacy of local housing they *can* apply to create an additional or selective licensing scheme. As time goes by, I fully expect that most local authorities will have licensing schemes for a huge percentage of all shared housing.

Again, I know this can sound like gobbledegook but remember, this legislation has to be complex because people are complex, as are who they rent from and what they rent, which creates such a hotchpotch of circumstances that no single straight answer is possible. I can give you the basics, the rest is up to you.

# You have a responsibility to keep yourself safe

I know I keep doing this, but here are yet more sources of information. Visit www.communities.gov.uk and work through the links on Private Rented Housing and Housing Act 2004. Again the residential landlords website is useful – they explain things very carefully to their members www.rla.org.uk or Shelter's website has some interesting information. Most university accommodation services will be as up to date as anyone can be on this as students were one of the most vulnerable groups created by this judgment. Alternatively, if you're at all concerned about the condition of your current shared unit, ring the Environmental Health Department at your local council. Every single member of staff has had extra training in this specific area to help *you*.

I apologise that I have to keep directing you elsewhere, but there are some very practical reasons.

1. The legislation is barely up and running yet and will take a couple of years to begin having real impact as we track how it's used nationally.

2. Tenants could really do with dedicated guides for both the new deposit system and the new HMO regulations – both of which I suspect the government will soon do – they have an excellent track record for user friendly booklets. Keep a look out online or call the booklet helpline periodically: **0870 1226 236**. I already see a new product code 05 HD0339 available, which should help you.

3. For reasons I won't bore you with, there is, from April 2006, no one size fits all safety requirement package that we landlords are used to. From April 2006, any unit raising concern will need to be individually assessed by an EHO using a complex safety formula known as HHSRS.

## *Why is safety in shared accommodation such a big deal?*

Because multiplying occupants multiplies risk. Four people cooking four meals at four different times has four times the potential for danger – multiply occupied properties that fall into the scope of these new rules will have some fairly tight regulations about overall conditions. They will not accept overcrowding. And many more landlords will need a licence to operate. The statistics I used earlier speak for themselves.

Sadly, I frequently hear cases where Environmental Health Departments try to take action against this type of housing and get little support from the tenants, who seem quite happy to accept accommodation if it is convenient. This is a bit like being happy to drive a car with bad brakes. Everything's fine until you *need* to stop.

### Some sensible advice

If you're worried about whether or not your own landlord ought to be improving safety, get on the phone to the local authority (Environmental Health Department) and ask. Call the CAB and ask.

Most of you know perfectly well if circumstances have forced you into taking a unit where the landlord doesn't give a damn about safety. Did they show you a gas safety certificate? Is the furniture safe? Does he provide paperwork/inventories? Has he shoved so many of you in a three-bedroom semi that the walls are bulging? Anything else that concerns you? Get on the phone. Lettings can be a tough old business – learn to help the authorities who spend entire careers trying to keep you safe.

---

**WARNING ANECDOTE**

Sadly missed, John Peel did a series of shows on the work of Environmental Health Officers to highlight their work called *A Life of Grime*. One show featured 13 students all trying to live in a small semi in London. Yup, that's not a typing error – 13. Up and down the country as workers move around for low waged work, many are 'hot bedding' property – sleeping in shifts to save money. There always were and always will be exploitative landlords.

It's your job as a tenant to make sure that *you are safe*!

## Unfit property

If you are living now, or have recently been living in, any property which you would like to report to the authorities, but dare not do so, here is some advice. Once you have left, but *only when you have received your deposit return,* write a letter detailing your concerns and post it (even anonymously) to the Environmental Health Department of your local council. They will, with a written complaint, usually inspect promptly.

> If *every* tenant living in unsafe or unfit accommodation reported it to the Environmental Health Department at their local council, even after they had left, the number of these units would nosedive. Remember, *you* may have found something better, but some other poor devil has just moved in.

Many times these type of properties are *wholly unknown to the authorities.* How can they know if tenants don't tell them? Overcrowding landlords certainly aren't going to. Some can keep a remarkably low profile if declaring their business will cost them cold hard cash for safety upgrades – let alone notify the taxman.

And on that note, I'll close. Remember to read the Appendices for a quick run through.

# Appendix 1

# Checklist of dos and don'ts

## Do

- Check carefully where you want to live, and for how long, before you sign leases.

- Do all your sums carefully, and be sure you can afford the total cost before you sign up.

- Check at least basic safety in your own accommodation.

- Remember, you take the property 'as seen', don't ask for a string of improvements unless they are safety related.

- Make sure you have the money available for the deposit, advance rent and all other advance charges before you agree to take a property.

- Register for council tax, water, electricity, gas, etc. Check meters when you move in and when you move out and *keep records*.

- Get an exemption certificate from your college if you are a student exempt from council tax. Don't just not pay it, you'll end up with a summons that way.

- Check that your own possessions are insured, your landlord's policy probably won't cover them.

- Report anything that breaks down immediately, and in writing if necessary.

- Be reliable with your rent, and keep a record of all payments.

- Replace anything that you have damaged or broken.

- Look after your landlord's property, remember you are only renting its use.

- Make sure your guests behave.

## Don't

■ Hand over any money unless you're certain you want a particular property.

■ View properties alone unless absolutely unavoidable and never ever without telling someone else where you are going and when.

■ Authorise builders, plumbers, etc to carry out work to the property without written consent, your landlord will probably refuse to reimburse you.

■ Do any damage and try to pretend you're not liable.

■ Imagine no one will know you live there and hope you won't have to pay your way. Most landlords and agents notify every service provider anyway.

■ Give keys or copies of keys to anyone else.

■ Invite your boy/girlfriend to live with you without your landlord's consent. The property was only let to the signatories of the lease, and you cannot invite others in to share the place or to help pay the rent.

■ Change the people living on joint tenancies without notifying the management. You may end up with no lease at all.

# Appendix 2

# Useful tips

Having read this guide, it must now be obvious that every part of the letting process is interdependent on the other. Choosing the right property and knowing what to look for in a good landlord are perhaps the most important of the choices you are trying to make. Many of the problems of poor conditions, unsafe properties, or unfair deposit retentions have the same core of agents and landlords in common. You might find the following suggestions useful.

- Ring the nearest local authority and ask if they have lists of approved landlords – many do and they can be a godsend for those on tight budgets.

- Student accommodation services will provide lists of accommodation for sharers, but not all universities insist their landlords have the same standards required by your local council.

- Ask outgoing tenants what the landlord is like before you move in. Pop back in the evening when the landlord or agent isn't around, the answer could be very interesting and it is usually well worth the trouble.

- If your friends or acquaintances like their landlord or their agent, take the phone number. Many of the best have discreet waiting lists or choose tenants by recommendation, for obvious reasons. Some of the best landlords rarely have to advertise at all.

- If you're looking to rent a room in a house, consider choosing one where the owner actually lives. Your legal rights may be limited, but the building is more likely to be safe. Many of the worst fire traps have absent landlords who live in a nice safe place up the road!

- If problems with the conduct of your landlord or tenant do arise after you have moved in, *take advice*. Don't just struggle on hoping things will get better, they may get worse. Find out where you stand, even six months can be a very long time with problematic management.

# Appendix 3

# Basic safety

Here is a list of basic safety tips and hints which you might consider before you make your choices on where to live.

- Make sure that all upholstered furniture has a British Standard label.

- Never take a rented property which doesn't have gas safety certificates for the appliances. Also check out these warning signs and avoid like the plague: old style gas water-heaters in the bathroom or kitchen; a smell of fumes from any gas appliance; soot or staining on or near any part of the gas fire or a boiler.

- Never try to save money by blocking ventilation grilles, they have often been installed to supply your gas appliance with sufficient air for safety.

- Don't take property where portable gas or paraffin heaters are provided, especially as your only source of heating.

- Look for smoke alarms, professionally installed fire alarms, fire extinguishers and fire blankets in kitchens.

- In large buildings look for fire alarms in hallways, fire doors which have a self closer on them so they close automatically behind you and fire extinguishers.

- Look for old electrical services and appliances. Do the lights flicker? Are there old style sockets? Do the heaters or kettles have old cables, or bare bits of wire?

There is now considerable publicity about gas safety certificates, and gas safety generally. What is often far less well publicised is that you can be equally poisoned by carbon monoxide from coal and smokeless fuel, even wood. So a solid fuel boiler that isn't required to have a special certificate can still be a problem. It's also a great deal more difficult to see signs of dangerous sooting on a fire, because you expect it to a greater extent.

Here are a few symptoms of carbon monoxide poisoning which could alert you to a problem: tiredness, drowsiness, headaches, dizziness and nausea.

If you are concerned, you must report to your landlord or agent *that day*. Do not use any appliance you are worried about until it has been checked. You can buy small domestic carbon monoxide testers to use at home if you are in any way concerned. They cost around £20 each and are a wise investment as they last years and you can take them with you when you move.

# Appendix 4

# Deposit return letters

(Only for rental deposits taken *before* April 2007.)

One of the single largest areas of dispute between landlords and tenants is that of deposit returns. This can be difficult for well-meaning tenants, who do everything that they imagine is required and still don't receive a deposit return after vacating the property. Now although the Tenancy Deposit Schemes (TDSs) will soon be running (making letters like these obsolete) this will still leave tens of thousands of tenants where deposits taken before 6 April 2007 are still held by landlords/agents. Until the deposit is safeguarded under a TDS, tenants may still have difficulty recovering their money.

Two letters are provided in this appendix to help tenants in this situation. The first letter is a polite request for a refund, showing what to mention and that the tenant should ask for the interest on their deposit to which they are entitled. The second is a more formal demand for a refund, to be used by tenants who are, as is all too common, being ignored.

Follow the instructions and fill in the blanks. If you are entitled to a refund, knowing what to say, when and to whom is very useful. While a landlord with good cause will happily go to court over the issue, less scrupulous landlords often perceive your deposit as additional income and are reluctant to return it. Well-informed tenants are less likely to fall victim to this quite unacceptable practice.

## First deposit return letter

Tenant's name
Tenant's address

Name of landlord or agent
Address of landlord or agent

Date

Dear (fill in)

re: (fill in the full address of the property you have vacated)

I was a tenant in the above property from (insert date) to (insert date). You held during my tenancy a deposit against damage amounting to (insert amount held as deposit).

I vacated the property as agreed, and returned the property in the condition required. I enclose (list here any receipts you have in connection with your final cleaning, if any - keep originals safe).

I enclose for your attention photocopies of my paid final receipts covering gas, electricity, telephone, water rates and council tax (add any other accounts which you have paid).

I should be grateful if you could arrange for my deposit, together with the interest now due on the monies held by yourself for the period of my tenancy to be posted to me at my new address above, at your earliest convenience.

Yours sincerely
(Your signature)

(Your name)

Send the letter to the landlord or agent *recorded delivery* ten days after vacation, and don't forget to enclose the copies of receipts referred to in the letter.

## Second deposit return letter

---

Tenant's name
Tenant's address

Name of landlord or agent
Address of landlord or agent

Date

Dear (fill in)

re: (fill in the address of the property you have vacated)

I refer to my letter of the (fill in date of first letter), to which I have received no reply despite recording its delivery.

You have by now been provided with all the necessary documentation to enable you to release my deposit, but have failed thus far to do so. The sum currently outstanding is (fill in amount of deposit), plus the accrued interest to the date of this letter.

I must now formally advise you that, both on moving into the property and on vacation of the same I took the precaution of (here outline in detail the precautions you took to safeguard your deposit, either the witnesses you had, or your recorded envelope of unopened proof — see Chapter 5 for ideas).

Unless therefore you have evidence to the contrary, I should be most obliged if you could now repay my deposit, in full and without further delay. Please send me receipts for any deductions you have made, plus a full written statement of the reasons for any such deductions.

Unless I am in receipt of all outstanding monies within seven days from the date of this letter I reserve the right, without further notice, to initiate a summons for their recovery through the Small Claims Court.

Yours sincerely
(Your signature)

(Your name)

---

Post this to the landlord or agent *recorded delivery* seven days after the first letter.

# Index

**Also by Lesley Henderson**

**The Landlord's Survival Guide**
The *truly practical insiders* handbook for *all* private landlords

This concise but comprehensive guide is for first-time – as well as established – landlords.

It is divided into Lessons, each of which is jam-packed with detail and insider tips. Most Lessons will only take a few minutes to read (although a few earlier ones take a little more) and each Lesson tells you exactly what you need to do – and why – to get the best results.

- Viewings: how to arrange and conduct them.
- Making a realistic rent assessment before spending any money.
- Knowing what agents should charge and should do.
- Advertising – how to write, where to place, and how to respond to callers – plus using the response to assess tenants.
- Selecting tenants and closing the deal.
- Deposits – explaining the new legislation.
- Agreeing Inventories, Schedules of Condition, and Property Profiles.
- Assured Shorthold Leases: what they are, the exceptions, and where to buy them for a song.
- Ending tenancies the easy, and the hard way.
- The legal responsibilities that no landlord can ignore.
- Particular aspects about Houses in Multiple Occupation.
- Property maintenance realistic costs and useful advice.
- Dealing with the tax man.

Each Lesson has tips, skills, time-management ideas, and problem solving advice, plus supportive guidance and helpful websites and phone numbers.

If you're looking for a bit of straight talking about your investment, or you're sufficiently interested to discover how to increase your own bottom line rather than some agent's, then this is the guide for you.

ISBN 978-1-84528-961-0

## Other Titles from How To Books

### The Beginner's Guide to Property Investment
The ultimate handbook for first-time buyers and would-be property investors
*Tony Booth*

This book provides an insight into many key issues; it explains what constitutes a sound investment, how you can examine your borrowing potential and create a golden credit rating, what mortgages are available and which are most suitable. It also discusses alternative property investment; buy-to-let, let-to-buy, renovation, buying property abroad, self-build and self-employed business enterprise; and shares generous amounts of inside information and well-kept trade secrets.

'It is true that there is a growing trend and an ever-expanding ability to buy property, but there is associated with it a mountainous capacity for critical mistakes. This book is intended for savvy investors who wish to evade such errors. By following the advice laid out in this book, conducting a thorough personal assessment, investigating properties worthy of purchase and exploring all the alternatives, you will find yourself able to buy a dwelling that meets your needs and one that provides financial security for the future.'

*Tony Booth*

ISBN 978-1-84528-961-0

**How To Build Your Own Home**
The ultimate guide to managing a self-build project and creating your dream house
*Tony Booth and Mike Dyson*

This book will guide you through the fundamental elements of the self-build programme, from identifying and assessing a suitable building plot to arranging finance and contractors. It deals with architects and designers, surveyors, labourers and tradesmen. It explains how to obtain planning permission and where to find appropriate insurance protection whilst construction is underway. Essentially, this book provides you with the know-how you need to complete a successful self-build project.

'Here you will find the practical knowledge required to go beyond your aspirations, to take that first step and start building the perfect home. At the end of the day, you will acquire the home you want, rather than one forced upon you from a limited variety, designed and constructed by a builder whose only motivation is to profit from your purchase. Instead of having to fit into a house, you can finally make a house fit you!'

*Tony Booth and Mike Dyson*

ISBN 978-1-84528-192-2

**Getting the Builders In**
A step-by-step guide to supervising your own building projects
*Leonard Sales*

'Undertaking a building or renovation project can be daunting, but this book provides everything you need to know in an easy to follow step-by-step guide.' – *Period Ideas*

'The author's plain speaking style has produced a clear guide through a potential minefield, which will give you the confidence to have the builders do what you want when you want.' – *Sean O'Neill, Managing Director Harry Neal (City) Ltd*

'Aimed at the lay client this book gives a practical step-by-step insight on matters that even experts in this field frequently fail to appreciate.' – *Jeremy F Emmett FRICS*

ISBN 978-1-84528-088-8

**How To Buy a Flat**

*Liz Hodgkinson*

'A must for flat buyers.' – *Index Magazine*

Buying a flat to live in or to let is different from buying and living in a house. For example, apartments are sold leasehold rather than freehold which means you buy a length of tenure rather than the property itself. This can have serious implications when the freeholder suddenly hikes up the service charges or lands you with a six-figure sum for exterior decoration. And more quarrels and lawsuits arise among flat-dwellers than with any other type of housing. This book explains the complicated leasehold laws governing flats and gives expert advice on how to live amicably in an apartment building.

ISBN 978-1-84528-115-1

## How To Buy and Let A Holiday Cottage
*Allison Lee*

This book gives a step-by-step guide to investing in a second home. It will show you how to: source the right property; prepare your property for letting; market your property; decide whether to use the services of an agent; take bookings and deal with cancellations; maintain and clean the property; receive guests; and deal with the financial aspect of running a holiday let business.

ISBN 978-1-84528-122-9

## Investing in a Second Home
*Wendy Pascoe*

This book provides a step-by-step guide to investing in a second home, whether for long lets, holiday lets, or buying for sons or daughters at university.

'...looks at the practical side of investing in property. Written by former BBC journalist, Wendy Pascoe, the book concentrates on raising funds, managing long lets and building a property portfolio.'
— *Show House*

ISBN 978-1-84528-138-0